HAUNTED FIELD GUIDE SERIES II

FIELD GUIDE
TO SPIRIT
PHOTOGRAPHY
BY DALE KACZMAREK

- A Ghost Research Society Press Publicatio

BOOKS BY DALE KACZMAREK

Windy City Ghosts (2000)
Windy City Ghosts II (2001)

Original Cover Artwork Designed by
Larry E. Arnold (author of "Ablaze")
Visit www.ParaScience.com

This Book is Published by
- Ghost Research Society Press -
A Division of the Ghost Research Society
PO Box 205 - Oak Lawn, Illinois - 60454
(708)425-5163
Visit us on the Internet at www.ghostresearch.org

First Printing - May 2002

ISBN: 0-9766072-3-9

Printed in the United States of America

THE HAUNTED FIELD GUIDE SERIES

Welcome to the next book in the Field Guide series from Ghost Research Society Press that will be dedicated to providing readers with short but concise information to not only haunted places, but to ghost research as well. The brain-child of Jim Graczyk, author of "A Field Guide to Chicago Hauntings", the books to come will take you beyond the cities and provide detailed listings, maps and directions to haunted places all over the Midwest and America. We also plan to devote books to various types of ghost research, investigations and much more!

We hope that you enjoy this new series and that you will journey with us in future editions.

Happy Hauntings!

- TABLE OF CONTENTS -

INTRODUCTION

Not since the early experiments of Sir William Crookes and other contemporary spirit photographers has so much attention and interest been devoted to spirit photography - the ability of capturing an elusive phantom image on photographic film. Science has come very far since those early camera and photographic techniques; yet, ordinary people continue to take strange and unusual images (sometimes with very inexpensive cameras) without realizing it. Their first thoughts are usually that something must be amiss with their camera or that the film is either defective or not properly developed or handled by the laboratory. Hence, the dismissal of yet another piece of evidence of spirit survival.

I have been utterly fascinated and intrigued by spirit photographs for over twenty years now. Thousands of alleged spirit photographs have come through the headquarters of the Ghost Research Society since it's conception in 1982. The flow has only increased with the advent of the Internet and email attachments. While the vast majority of these photographs are simply misinterpretation of the facts, they continue to come to my attention in increasing numbers.

The first spirit images were documented with old, antiquated devices. However, *camera obscuras* were the first such device used for picture-taking purposes.. The Camera Obscura (Latin for Dark room) was a dark box or room with a hole in one end. If the hole was small enough, an inverted image would be seen on the opposite wall.

Such a principle was known by thinkers as early as Aristotle (c. 300 BC). It is said the Roger Bacon invented the camera obscura just before the year 1300, but this has never been accepted by scholars; more plausible is the claim that he used one to observe solar eclipses. In fact, the Arabian scholar Hassan ibn Hassan (also known as Ibn al Haitam), in the 10th century, described what can be called a camera obscura in his writings; manuscripts of his observations are to be found in the India Office Library in London, England.

In his essay "On the Form of the Eclipse" he wrote:

"The image of the sun at the time of the eclipse, unless it is total, demonstrates that when its light passes through a narrow, round hole and is cast on a plane opposite to the hole, it takes on the form of a moon-sickle.

The image of the sun shows the peculiarity only when the hole is very small. When the hole is enlarged, the picture changes..... ."

The earliest record of uses of a camera obscura can be found in the writings of Leonardo da Vinci (1452-1519). At about the same period Daniel Barbaro, a Venetian, recommended the camera as an aid to drawing and perspective. He wrote:

"Close all shutters and doors until no light enters the camera except through the lens, and opposite hold a piece of paper, which you move forward and backward until the scene appears in the sharpest detail. There on the paper you will see the whole view as it really is, with its distances, its colours and shadows and motion, the clouds, the water twinkling, the birds flying. By holding the paper steady you can trace the whole perspective with a pen, shade it and delicately colour it from nature."

In the mid sixteenth century Giovanni Battista della Porta (1538-1615) published what is believed to be the first account of the possibilities as an aid to drawing. It is said that he made a huge "camera" in which he seated his guests, having arranged for a group of actors to perform outside so that the visitors could observe the images on the wall. The story goes, however, that the sight of up-side down performing images was too much for the visitors; they panicked and fled, and Battista was later brought to court on a charge of sorcery!

Though Battista's account is wrapped up in a study of the occult, it is likely that from that time onwards many artists will have used a camera obscura to aid them in drawing, though either because of the association with the occult, or because they felt that in some way their artistry was lessened, few would admit to using one. Several are said to have used them; these include Giovanni Canale - better known as Canaletto (1697-1768), Vermeer (1632-1675), Joshua Reynolds (1723-1792), and Paul Sandby (1725-1809), a founding member of the Royal Academy.

Though some, including Joshua Reynolds, warned against the indiscriminate use of the camera obscura, others, notably, Algarotti, a writer on art and science and a highly influential man amongst artists, strongly advocated its use in his Essays on Painting (1764):

"the best modern painters among the Italians have availed

themselves of this contrivance; nor is it possible that they should have otherwise represented things so much to the life....Let the young painter, therefore, begin as early as possible to study these divine pictures...

Painters should make the same use of the Camera Obscura, which Naturalists and Astronomers make of the microscopes and telescope; for all these instruments equally contribute to make known, and represent Nature."

About the same time, the lens was being developed. Once again Roger Bacon's name is associated with this as some have claimed that it was he who invented spectacles. Gerolomo Cardano (1501-1576), an Italian mathematician, introduced a glass disc in place of a pinhole in his camera, and Barbaro also used a convex lens. Why the name lens? It is claimed that because Italian lenses were by-convex, they seemed to resemble the brown lentils they used to make soup - so the lens came from the Latin for lentil.

The first cameras were enormous. Athanasius Kircher (1601-1680) in a book written in 1646, described one that consisted of an outer shell with lenses in the center of each wall.

It had an inner shell containing transparent paper for drawing; the artist needed to enter by a trapdoor. Other versions also appeared. Sedan chairs were converted, and tent-type cameras were also in use - even up to the beginning of the 1900s. Then smaller, portable ones were made. Thus the camera obscura, as it came to be known, became a popular aid to sketching.

Between 1816-26, Joseph Nicephore Niepce became the first person to achieve a photographic image with a camera obscura; and so the camera was developed.

The first spirit images on photographic plates, however, were thought to have been accidental. It did raise the general public's interest and many flocked to get their picture taken with the deceased. Some photographers came under intense scrutiny and even public disgrace for faking spirit photographs, as much money could be made in this venture.

In the present, while photographing the family picnic, a graduation or thousands of other possible innocent situations, the farthest thing from one's mind is the possibility of photographing a ghost or entity. It is for this reason alone that thousands of possible vital bits of collective evidence are tossed out as trash. As a person with a keenly trained eye and knowledge in spirit photography, I look at this "trash" in a different light.

In the pages ahead, I intend to arm you with the necessary information to better your chances of capturing a spirit with your camera, whether it be a disposable camera or a very expensive 35mm. The following chapters will document the history of spirit photography and examine those early pioneers of the art including Crookes, Boursnell, Buguet, Mumler and Parkes. After that, the basics of camera operation will be discussed, including all the different varieties of cameras currently available today and the different kinds of films that can be used, including the highly interesting but difficult to use, infrared. Digital cameras, camcorders and digital camcorders will be touched upon due to the great amount of strange video images that have come to my attention over the years especially from the Sony Nightvision cameras.

There will also be many examples of spirit photography that have been taken by myself, by members of the Ghost Research Society and by ordinary people. As, as I have already mentioned, many natural explanations can sometimes arise from picture-taking. These will be thoroughly looked at including camera straps, cigarette smoke or steam coming from the photographer's mouth due to the difference in temperature, bad film, reflections, etc. I will attempt to show you how you can analyze your own images using computer software available for purchase and your own common sense and most importantly; how to properly attempt spirit photography. This will include the safeguards and controls you should employ so as not to accidentally capture a natural image on your film.

It is my hope to educate you in the proper methodology and give you tips that have worked for myself and members of the Ghost Research Society in the past. As I've stated in the past, there are no "experts" in the field nor do I claim to be one myself. I will simply give you information, arm you with the proper tools, film and situations and hope for the best possible results. The methods that you will read about have been tried and tested over almost 20 years of research and have yielded some great results for me and I hope they will work good for you as well.

If you do happen to photograph something unusual through these methods, I would very much be interested in seeing a copy. You can mail it directly to me at the Ghost Research Society, PO Box 205, Oak Lawn, IL. 60454-0205 or send it as an email attachment to dalekaczmarek@comcast.net

Happy hauntings and Good Luck!

Dale Kaczmarek
Spring 2002

I. HISTORY OF SPIRIT PHOTOGRAPHY

Spirit photography is defined as the production of photographs on which alleged spirit forms are visible. When the plate is developed there appears, in addition to the likeness of the sitter, a shape resembling more or less distinctly the human form, which at the time of the exposure was imperceptible to the normal vision.

The practice of spirit photography originated in America some years ago and has enjoyed a fitful existence to the present day. It was first discovered by William H. Mumler of Boston, Massachusetts . He was the head engraver of the jewelry firm Bigelow, Kennard & Co. of Boston. One day in 1862, a Dr. Gardner was photographed by Mumler and on the plate appeared an image which the Gardner identified as his cousin, who had died twelve years before. Dr. Gardner published abroad his experience and the new photography was at once adopted by spiritualists who saw it a means of proving life after death.

Among the first to investigate Mumler's powers was Andrew

Jackson Davis, editor of the *Herald Progress* in New York. Davis first sent a professional photographer to test Mumler and on his favorable report conducted an investigation himself. Davis found the new psychic manifestation genuine. It apparently did not matter whether Mumler worked in his own studio or in that of others, whether he used his own chemicals or not.

In 1863, however, Dr. Gardner discovered that in at least two instances a living model had sat for Mumler's "spirit" pictures. Though he continued to believe that some of the photographs might be genuine, his exposure of Mumler's fraud effectively checked the movement for a time.

After the lapse of some six years, Mumler appeared this time in New York, where the authorities endeavored to prosecute him, but the evidence against him was insufficient to prove fraud, and he was acquitted. He eventually died in poverty in 1884.

W. H. MUMLER.

William Mumler

The legal action taken against Mumler cast doubt on future alleged spirit photographs and photographers, even though many more followed in Mumler's shoes. People of the time sincerely wished it were true and that these spirit photographs were proof of an afterlife.

A Mr. and Mrs. Guppy, well-known spiritual mediums of the time, tried without success to produce spirit photographs in private, and finally called in the aid of a professional photographer, Mr. Hudson. A photograph taken by Hudson of Mr. Guppy now revealed a dim, draped spirit form. Hudson immediately became popular and his studio was largely patronized as Mumler's had been earlier.

Mr. Thomas Slater, a London-based optician, made careful observations of his process without being able to detect any fraud. Mr. Beattie, a professional photographer of the time, and something of a skeptic, made the following statement concerning Hudson's performances:

"They were not made by double exposure, nor by figures projected in space in any way; they were not the result of mirrors; they were not produced by any machinery in the background, behind it, above it, or below it, nor by any contrivance connected with the bath, the camera, or the camera-slide."

Mr. Traill Taylor, editor of the British Journal of Photography said that *"at no time during the preparation , exposure or development of the pictures was Mr. Hudson within ten feet of the camera or dark room. Appearances of an abnormal kind did certainly appear on several plates."*

Such testimonies would naturally seem to raise spirit photography to the level of a genuine psychic phenomenon. But a careful analysis of the evidence, such as is given by Mrs. Sidgwick in her article of Spirit Photography in the Psychical Research Society's Proceedings, vol. VII, will serve to show how even a trained investigator may be deceived by sleight-of-hand. It is also notable that Mr. Beattie himself pointed out instances of double exposure in Hudson's productions. In spite of this, Hudson continued to practice and various spiritualist magazines continued to lend him their support, with the exception of the *Spiritualist,* whose editor himself a practical photographer, had aided Mr. Beattie in the denunciation of spirit photography.

Mr. Beattie himself also attempted to produce spirit images and succeeded in obtaining vague blotches and flaws on his pictures, some of them bearing a dim resemblance to a human figure.

In 1874 E. Buguet, a Frenchman traveled to London where he too began a career in spirit photography. Most of his photographs represented well-known personages. Many of his pictures were recognized by his clients, and even when he had been tried by the French Government and had admitted deception, there were those who refused to regard his confession as spontaneous and inclined to the opinion that he had been bribed by the Jesuits to confess to fraud of which he was innocent. He was imprisoned for one year and fined 500 francs.

In his confession he stated that his spirit photographs were produced by double exposure. First he dressed up his assistants to play the part of the ghost, later he constructed a doll which, variously draped, served in a similar manner for the body of the ghost. This figure, and a large stock of heads were seized by the police at his studio.

Rev. Stainton Moses, a famous medium, was convinced that at least some of Buguet's spirit photographs were genuine. He said that the prosecution bore traces of clerical origin, that the judge was biased and Buguet must have been bribed or terrorized to confess and to manufacture a boxful of trick apparatus.

Camille Flammarion (1842-1925), famous astronomer, author and psychic researcher, was convinced that Buguet cheated. In *Mysterious Psychic Forces* he writes that Buguet *"having allowed me to experiment with him, let me conduct my researches for five weeks before I detected his fraudulent methods and mechanism. While I was pushing my investigation a little farther I saw with my own eyes Buguet's prepared negatives."*

Richard Boursnell (1832-1909) was an English spirit photographer who allegedly obtained psychic markings on his plates as early as 1851, but being accused by his partner of spoiling the plates, he stopped taking photographs himself until some forty years later. A repetition of the same annoyance occurred again. W.T. Stead swore that the markings were psychic and prevailed upon Boursnell to sit for spirit photographs. He was strikingly successful and in 1903 the spiritualists of London presented him with a signed testimonial and a purse of gold as a mark of their high esteem. A hundred chosen spirit photographs were put on exhibition in the rooms of the Psychological Society at Portman Square. Of course, he too, faded into obscurity.

A bit later, another English spirit photographer, F.M. Parkes, who, in the association with M. Reeves, the proprietor of a dining room, obtained recognized spirit extras after three months of experiments in 1872, the same year Hudson had also been successful. Without the presence of Reeves or his own wife, Parkes could not get full forms or clearly defined images, but only white patches and cloudy appearances. In accordance with spirit directions he set it as a condition to have the plates in his possession in the dark room previous to their being placed in the camera for purposes of magnetization. To avert suspicion he had a hole cut in the dark room through which the sitters could see the plate through its entire process.

Dr. Sexton wrote enthusiastically of Parkes' powers in the *Christian Spiritualist*. Stainton Moses gave the following interesting description in *Human Nature*: *"A considerable number of the earlier pictures taken by Parkes and Reeves were allegorical. One of the earliest, taken in April 1872, shows Mr. Reeves' father holding up a cross above his head and displaying an open book on which is written 'Holy Bible'. Another shows a cloud of light covering two-thirds of the pictures, and flashes of light, with a distinct cross in the centre. Another, in which Mr. and Mrs. Everitt were the sitters, taken June 8, 1872, is a symbolical picture of a very curious nature. Mr. Everitt's head is surrounded with a fillet on which 'Truth' is inscribed, while three pencils of light dart up from it. There are at least two figures in the picture which blot out Mrs. Everitt altogether...."*

Sir William Crookes (1832-1919) was one of the greatest physicists of the century and was Elected Fellow of the Royal Society in 1863, Royal Gold Medal 1875, Davy Medal 1888, Sir Joseph Copley Medal 1904, knighted in 1897, Order of Merit 1910 and President at different times of the Royal Society, the Chemical Society, the Institution of Electrical Engineers, the British Association and the Society for Psychical Research. He discovered the element Thallium, invented the radiometer, spinthariscope and Crookes tubes. He was also fascinated with psychic phenomena and spirit photography. He was obsessed with the famous psychic D.D. Home and followed his exploits throughout his lifetime; later becoming involved with seances and the manifestations of Katie King through psychic Florence Cook.

The story of Florence Cook and Katie King, her constant companion, read like a fairy tale. Point by point Crookes grappled with the great problem; to establish the separate existence of the two girls. He measured the difference in height, noted the absence of a blister on Katie's neck, the absence of perforation in Katie's ears, the difference in complexion, in bodily proportion, manner and expression. He had himself photographed with Katie King and Florence Cook in the same position and while his picture completely tallied in the two photographs the discrepancy between the girls was well observable.

Katie and Miss Cook were seen together by eight people besides Crookes. Forty-two photographs were taken. Altogether they bore out marked differences between the medium and the apparition. No matter what extensive precautions were employed by Crookes, the results, in the eyes of skeptics, were always not evidential.

Long after the death of Crooks, rumors circulated that Florence Cook had been his mistress, and Crooks had connived at fraud in order to carry on the affair with her. These accusations were presented in the book *The Spiritualists* by Trevor Hall, London, 1962 (Garrett-Helix, New York, 1963), and the article "William Crookes and the Psychical Phenomena of Mediumship" by R.G. Medhurst and K.M. Goldney (*Proceedings of the S.P.R.,* London, vol. 54, pt. 195, March 1964). There is, however, no reliable evidence for such rumors, which are highly speculative.

One of the most striking spirit photographs was produced by William Walker, the first man to obtain psychic extras in color in the Crewe Circle of William T. Stead on May 6, 1912, 22 days after the latter's death on the *Titanic.* Walker visited Stead in September 1911 to show him his album of psychic photographs. Stead desired that Walker should "keep him posted" in regard to future success. He did not get in touch with him afterwards and when the tragedy of the *Titanic* became known his wife told him:

"You promised to keep Mr. Stead posted, but now it is too late."

Walker replied, *"Possibly he will comprehend why I did not write to him and send him copies as I promised but he will perhaps try to keep me posted."*

On May 6, 1912, Walker sat in Crewe for psychic photography. Strict test conditions were made, own plates used, one double dark slide. Surrounded by a white nebulous mass a very clear photograph of W.T. Stead was obtained with a circular inscription: *"Dear Mr. Walker, I will try to keep you posted, W.T. Stead."* The message was in Stead's handwriting which Miss Harper, Stead's secretary, found undoubtedly genuine.

It does seem that a lot of the so-called 'early spirit photographers' resorted to some kind of fakery and fraud to make money and become known throughout the world. Many of them were exposed by their peers or debunkers of the time, while others were never caught and never resorted to alleged trickery. I'm sure that most of you have seen some of these early examples of spirit photography and compared to modern-day photographs, they appear laughable. They look phony and fraudulent by today's standards. But those of yesteryear truly believed that these images were nothing but genuine.

Most modern day spirit photographers employ more stringent safeguards to ensure that what they photograph is not explainable. However, the vast majority of spirit photographs come from the ordinary person. Someone who is simply photographing an innocent event such as a birthday party, social gathering, a vacation, wedding, graduation or just family photography. While not seeing anything while photographing the event or person, something sometimes does reveal itself either in the background or the foreground. It's usually something the photographer was sure wasn't there when he or she took the picture.

These images can vary from cloudy or misty formations, to streaks of light, balls or orbs, shadowy figures or even semi-transparent images that appear to look like either people, animals or inanimate objects. While a great many of these images can be explained, many can not. It's those images that don't have a readily identifiable explanation that are most intriguing to the ghost researcher.

Later I will go into more detail about the various ways that spirits can manifest on film and how you can discern if you have a natural or supernatural image in a developed print. For now let's explain the basics of camera operation and how images are obtained on photographic film or emulsion.

II. BASIC CAMERA OPERATION

One of the most important things a camera operator should remember, and know up front, is that a camera, no matter what kind of device is used, operates quite differently from the human eye, even though there is an analogy between the two.

The human eyelid can be compared to a shutter of the camera; opening and closing at various speeds from a quick wink to a longer length much like a camera operating at say 1/1000th of a second to a long time exposure. The cornea and lens of the eye work to focus the image being perceived by the individual much like the focus ring on a camera. The human eye does this job automatically, the camera, however can be either an auto-focus or manual-focus device. The iris of the human eye dilates to allow more or less light to be sent to the retina much as the diaphragm of the camera set to various F-stops reacts.

And, last, but not least, the actual retina deep inside the aqueous humor of the eyeball is what actual receives the image, similar to the photographic film inside a camera. The human eye processes the image immediately while the film must be sent to a camera shop or darkroom to be developed unless the operator is utilizing an Instamatic camera which develops the film in sixty seconds or less. This is where the analogy ends.

The images collected by the human eye are interpreted by the brain, the master computer, while the photographer can be influenced by his surroundings, emotions, senses, experiences and mood. Even experienced photographers can sometimes allow themselves to be influenced by some outside factor or factors.

The individual who is credited with the taking of the first genuine picture (if it can be assumed that to mean a permanent image produced by the direct action of light) was Joseph Nicephore Niepce in 1826 at Chalons-sur-Saone of his attic window. His first efforts were weak negatives on paper treated with silver chloride and poorly fixed with nitric acid. By 1822 he devised a method whereby an asphalt varnish (Bitumen of Judea) on glass with a mixture of oils to fix the image was used. Using this later process, he was able take a picture of the building from his workshop, which required an eight hour exposure!

Today sensitive material consists of two essential layers: an emulsion (light-sensitive silver salts suspended in gelatin) coated on a transparent base (usually made of acetate). Despite decades of progress by numerous photographers and developers, the photographic process is still dependent on the action of light on silver salts or "halides". When the light comes into contact with the film it affects the basic structure of these halides within the emulsion layer. When more light is introduced, more grains of halides are affected. However, it isn't until a chemical agent or 'developer' is employed that the latent image is finally revealed to the photographer.

This is accomplished by converting the halides that have been exposed to the incoming light into minute grains of pure metallic silver, which appear black. Those halides that were not affected or exposed to incoming light are left unaltered by the developer.

A negative image is produced in this fashion (negative because it is the light areas that have produced black silver). However the emulsion is still delicate and sensitive to further incoming light, so it is therefore necessary to fix the image by removing all the undeveloped halides. They are made water soluble by the fixer solution and washed away, leaving only stable metallic silver on clear film.

A camera basically consists of two items; a light-tight box and a lens. The lens is used to collect the light from the scene being photographed and focused into an image. The box must be light-tight to ensure that no other light is collected other then through the lens of the camera. However, cameras nowadays have many more features or luxuries that make picture taking easy even for the novice or amateur.

Shutters are simple timing devices that open and close to restrict the length of time that light is allowed to reach the film. However, another factor is also crucial to the exposure and that is controlled by the aperture. The aperture is a simple hole located just behind the lens of the camera; the bigger the hole, the brighter the image. This is what is known in the jargon as the F-stops. The larger the number, the smaller the aperture and therefore the smaller amount of light is allowed into the camera and vice versa. So F-22 allows much more light than an F-8 setting. A large aperture and a fast shutter speed can produce the equivalent exposure to a small aperture and a slow shutter speed. Today's modern auto-focus, fully automated cameras take care of everything from the aperture, F-stops, focusing to setting off the flash, when needed.

Light can be thought of as an infinite number of rays emanating or being reflected from every point on an object and traveling from it in straight lines. Because they travel randomly, something must be employed to control these "confused" rays and that job falls to the lens. Much like a prism, a lens bends incoming light rays, collecting and redirecting them. But unlike a prism, a lens is curved. Because of this curve, rays strike different parts of the lens and are bent in varying angles. In general, the thicker and more curved the surface is, the greater will be it's ability to bend the light. This is usually measured at its focal length; the distance from the center of the lens to the point at which parallel rays entering the lens converge. The more the light is bent, the shorter the focal length will be.

When the lens is focused at infinity, it is exactly one focal length away from its focal plane, where the image is formed. Therefore the operation of focusing involves moving the lens away from the focal plane to bring nearer objects into focus.

When a lens is focused on a point a certain distance away, there will be a zone both in front of and behind this point that also appears acceptably sharp on the film. This is referred to as depth of field.

Depth of field can be controlled because it is affected by changes in the aperture size (F-stops). When fully opened there is a small depth of field and the further it is "stopped" down, the depth of field increases. For purposes of composing a shot, photographers often select the aperture that gives the depth of field required and then match the shutter speed to produce the correct exposure.

Depth of field is useful in a number of ways other than for aesthetic effects. One is by affording the user to pre-focus the camera; a distinct advantage when it is known in advance that there will not be enough time to manually focus for a shot to be taken. This again, is only useful by those photographers who prefer to manually adjust for each and every picture. Newer cameras take the guess-work out of depth of field or unclear photographs by instantly sending out a beam of infrared light and calculating perfect depth of field, lighting and focus.

Shutters, as mentioned earlier, simply allow so much light to reach the camera by opening the closing from very slow speeds to extremely fast ones. Couple the fast shutter speeds and fast film such as 400 to 3200 ASA and you can quite literally freeze fast moving objects or take pictures under very low light conditions. The latter being accomplished through the light-gathering ability of the film being used.

The two most used type of cameras in today's market are the viewfinder and the single lens reflex camera.

The viewfinder camera actually uses a separate viewfinder,

which is not exactly what the camera or film actually sees. This is often called parallax and is the distance between the lens and the viewfinder, which the image in the viewfinder does not exactly coincide with the captured image. This is often more pronounced when the subject is close to the camera. This can result in classic accidents such as a person's head disappearing off the top of the picture or the subject not properly centered in the frame. And since this is not "what you see is what you get" obstructions are common such as a finger in front of the actual lens not seen through the viewfinder because it's not the exact same angle.

The single-lens reflex camera is the ultimate in picture-taking. The one lens serves for both viewing and taking the picture, therefore eliminating the problem of parallax. Most so-called accidents are now avoided through the use of this model of camera. It's much more versatile and has the ability to interchange a lens thereby further enhancing the picture-taking process. However, there are any number of equally great instamatic cameras on the market today that take equally great pictures with the point and shoot properties. The advantages with these cameras are immediately evident as the picture is developed within a minute, giving the photographer the ability to reshoot an image or site while still on the scene if the first picture was not to his liking.

The different types of cameras will be thoroughly discussed in the next chapter including the ancient 110/126 instamatic to the modern-day digital models. My likes and dislikes will be public record and while I suggest you experiment with them all, if possible, certain cameras, with a certain combination of films seems to work best for me. I'll point out which combinations are the most desirable.

Whether you use an expensive or relatively cheap disposable camera, there's always the possibility of getting a paranormal image on the developed film. Film, and the development process in general, is something that the amateur and seasoned professional alike should know about even though you might not be actively involved in that episode of photography.

III. CAMERAS AND FILMS

The 110 camera, also using 16mm film, had pre-loaded drop-in cartridges to suit the novice. Most of these early, easy-to-use cameras, had limited shutter speeds and were made for those who simply wished to point and shoot without the hassle of adjustments and manually loaded and winding of film.

The 126 or Brownie Instamatic, as it was sometimes called, was initially Kodak's earlier attempt at a cartridge-loading camera, though the designation of Instamatic led many people to assume it was an instant picture, rather than an instant load, camera. This format suffered from the same drawbacks as the 110 regarding choice of film, factory processing, and lack of accuracy in focusing due to the absence of a proper pressure plate, but the 126 transparencies are returned from processing in 5x5 cm mounts, the same size as 35mm film.

I examined quite a number of alleged spirit photographs in both of these formats. There are many limitations in both of these cameras and films, namely the lack of adjustment for focus, lighting and film speed. The film was sold in one standard speed and could not be pushed.

The nominal speed of a film is that which the manufacturer recommends for processing in a developer that gives optimum results. Processing in the more energetic developers, or in those which give finer grain, requires amendment either way to the film speed and effectively extends the film's versatility. Increasing of a film speed, say from 400 ASA to 800 ASA, with a corresponding increase in development time, is known as pushing.

Pushed negatives do not give optimum quality and the technique really works best with subjects under flat lighting conditions. It's recommended simply to use a faster film such as 1000 ASA or above for extremely low-light conditions, time exposures or attempted spirit photography. Current film speeds can be purchased up to 3200 ASA without having to push the film, thereby giving the photographer ample light-gathering ability while not having to worry about the developed quality of the finished photograph.

While some researchers might prefer a fast black and white film such as Tri-X, color films can also be used with good quality and sharpness. Usually the black and white film should have panchromatic sensitivity and high speed. Kodak Tri-X Pan film has a very fine grain and high speed (400 ASA). This film is unusually sensitive and somewhat shifted towards the Ultraviolet end of the spectrum and when coupled with black and white Infrared film, gives the photographer the widest range of both the visible and invisible spectrum.

While Kodak recommends that certain "special" films be shot in conjunction with barrier filters to absorb certain unwanted colors or spectrums, I suggest that no filter be used when attempting spirit photography. The argument is simple. Any filter placed on your camera restricts and stops certain colors and frequencies from reaching the film or emulsion. Since, at present, no one knows what frequency or color spectrum ghosts reside in, no filter should be used. You might, in actuality, be filtering out a ghostly presence through the use of a filter. The preferred method is allowing the total spectrum of light to strike the film, thereby giving the photographer a better chance of obtaining a paranormal image on the developed film. However, clear filters, sometimes called Sky Filters, should be used on 35mm cameras as they protect the valuable lens from becoming scratched from misuse or accidents. It's much cheaper to replace a filter costing only a couple of dollars rather than paying for an entire new lens which can reach into the hundreds of dollars for the major name brands.

Color film can be used in spirit photography just as black and white. However usually because the photographer or researcher is using his or her camera in subdued or low-light conditions such as a cemetery at night, a abandoned house or simply a dark room in an alleged haunted house, not much color might be evident on the finished product. Therefore, black and white is usually the preferred type of film. If something is found on the film of a paranormal nature, you would only have to distinguish between black, white and grey tones rather than the entire visible light color spectrum.

I have used Kodak Ektachrome 400 ASA film for many years now with varied success. When the 1000 speed film first came out, I eagerly stood in line to purchase a roll hoping to more than double the amount of light I could capture under low-light conditions. I was greatly disappointed because of the graininess of the film and never used it again. However, the film has since gone through improvements and it's now quite a good choice for those that wish to capture an image without the use of a flash.

Before I go on with the 35mm, another equally good camera for spirit photography should be mentioned here, the Polaroid instant camera. This camera develops an instant picture usually within 60 seconds in your hand. For all practical purposes instant picture cameras have eliminated the time gap between making an exposure and seeing the result.

The first model, and also the first camera using a diffusion transfer system for general photography, was introduced by Edwin Land in 1947. It produced sepia-toned positive prints in 60 seconds. Improvements quickly led to black and white prints and to a reduction in the processing time, in some cases 10 seconds!

Instant picture cameras have a number of obvious advantages over conventional 35mm types. The most beneficial is that if a photograph is not satisfactory another can be taken immediately. Also, a ghostly image can be immediately viewed and then the area can be re-shot again and with 35mm cameras with different kinds of film. It can be used as a "feeling ground" for possible paranormal activity. Many professional cameras take special Polaroid camera backs, allowing the use of instant film to check exposure and lighting balance before the actual shot.

After the exposure, the self-processing equipment takes over. The film comprises negative and positive materials, folded separately in a container that fits into the back of the camera. The developer is contained in pods sandwiched between the two. After the exposure is made, a tab of paper is pulled to bring negative and positive into contact. The photographer then pulls a second tab to draw positive and negative through the rollers, which squeeze the processing reagent between the two sheets. The negative is developed and the image migrates to the positive. After the development, usually sixty seconds, the positive is peeled away. However, the newer Polaroid cameras have taken the guess-work and counting out of the equation. Now the film simply exits the camera and immediately begins to develop fully.

On the standard instant picture cameras, exposure control is automatic and the camera is easy to operate. They are usually inexpensive and current models have built-in flashes rather than the older flashcubes or bulbs. They produce positive prints but no negatives. Copy negatives can, of course, be made at camera stores if additional prints are required or desired. The SX-70s soon followed in their footsteps.

My camera of choice in this category is the Polaroid Spectra 2 camera which has an aperture/shutter system from f/10 to f/45 and from 1/245th to 2.8 seconds. It weighs less than two pounds without a film pack and the film speed is approximately ISO 600. The disadvantages is that there is only 10 pictures per pack and the film is quite expensive when not on sale. The lens is a patented Quintic, three-element, 125mm system with ten-zone focusing from two feet to infinity. All ghostly arsenals should have some kind of instant picture camera at their disposal at all times! Polaroid, by far, makes the best in this field.

I have seen quite a number of excellent spirit photographs taken with this type of camera in the past! Most often captured types of images are cloudy images and discolorations, which I don't believe has anything to do with the film and/or weather conditions at the time. I highly recommend using this type of camera prior to shooting areas with digital or 35mm types.

However, by far the best, most reliable and flexible of the cameras out on the market today is the 35mm single lens reflex. They have become point and shoot in many aspects or others can be used completely manually, which allows the photographer to manipulate the shutter speeds and f-stops for maximum performance.

I have two Canon AE-1 SLR cameras at my disposal. The older of the two automatically selects the f-stops while you set the shutter speed. The other is completely automatic and selects both f-stops and shutter speeds. Of course, both of these can be used in the manual mode at any time for longer time-exposures or wider lens openings. This can be a plus when you are shooting in extremely low-light conditions or wish to keep the camera lens opened for light-gathering abilities.

My other camera of choice is a Cannon EOS RebelX S, which is auto-focus, auto-flash, auto-rewind and entirely automatic in regards to both shutter speeds and f-stops. The perfect camera for those quick shots you need to make, in case you actually see something with the naked eye and don't need to be fumbling with the manual settings.

The 35mm is by far the most versatile and successful design of camera. The SLR is the king of cameras! One lens serves both for viewing and taking the picture, thus overcoming the problem of parallax, and, because the viewfinder automatically shows the image exactly as it will be recorded, lenses are easily interchangeable. SLRs can be adapted to almost any task while remaining convenient for everyday work. However, a complex mechanism is needed to make an SLR function, and this brings certain obvious but minor disadvantages.

Most SLRs use 35mm film, but some large-format types, such as the Hasselblad and the Bronica, take roll-film producing off-sized negatives. The reflex mechanism consists of a mirror, set at an angle of 45 degrees just behind the lens, which reflects light up to form an image on the focusing screen. A focal plane shutter behind the mirror protects the film while the camera is focused. The image formed on the screen is upright but laterally reversed, and in some models this screen provides an optional waist-level viewing; for eye-level viewing (standard on almost all 35mm models) a 'pentaprism' housed directly above the screen reflects the image through the eyepiece and reverses it so that it is both upright and laterally correct.

To insure that the image on the screen is bright enough to allow accurate focusing and clear viewing, nearly all SLRs are fitted with an automatic diaphragm. Instead of closing down as soon as the aperture is turned, it remains fully open until the moment the picture is taken.

When the shutter release is depressed the camera performs a complex series of actions. First the diaphragm closes down to the preselected aperture; the mirror flips up out of the way, temporarily blacking out the viewing screen; the shutter then exposes the film at the selected speed and finally, in all but a few models, the mirror returns to its original position and the diaphragm reopens. In some older models, the mirror does not return until the film is wound for the next shot. Newer SLRs have auto-film advance.

The camera or cameras that you will eventually decide to use for your investigations or experiments ultimately depends on your budget and what you can afford. Not only is there the initial investment of the camera, but there is the added expense of film and development if you don't have access to a darkroom and are not knowledgeable enough to develop your own film, which can be tricky, somewhat expensive and time-consuming. There are also a number of optional devices and supplements that you will also need to add to your photography arsenal including flash units, tripods, light meters, cable releases, filters, etc. These will be discussed in length later on in the book. While you only might be able to afford something very inexpensive at first, go for it. You can always upgrade and buy a more expensive and far more reliable camera sometime in the future. The important point is to try to experiment with whatever you have at your disposal!

We have come a long way since those early spirit photographers of the last two centuries and it's become much more easier to take relatively good pictures for a modest amount of money. Now that you've selected your camera, the next question is what type of film you should use. Again this also depends on where you live, what type of stores there are in your area that sell film, your budget (again), your own knowledge of the various types of film currently available on the market and how complex your experiments and investigations need to be. And, lastly, who will develop the film for you. There's no use shooting high-speed Infrared film if there is no one nearby that can develop it for you and that's not the kind of film you would want to put into the U.S. Postal System!

I will next discuss the various kinds of film and their uses in the next chapter along with what worked best for me, what gave me good results and suggestions that you can put to practical use in your endeavors of capturing that elusive spirit on film.

IV. FILMS AND THEIR USES

The bulk of this chapter will concentrate on the films for use with the 35mm camera, as there is not a large selection of films for the lesser models; 110, 126 and Polaroid. If a 110 or 126 is all that your budget allows, you must pretty much resign yourself to using a single type of film which, if used in low-light conditions, will require a flash unit or flashcubes depending on the model. These instant-load cartridges are usually available in either 12 or 20-exposure length. Polaroids have a slightly better selection of films, including faster film for underlit conditions. But the problems still arise here because of the absence of shutter control and f-stop manipulation. A flash will be the only way to overcome shooting pictures in darkened homes and cemeteries at night and the possibility of getting a flash bounce or reflection off a tombstone or reflective surface in a home is always there. That's why the 35mm film is truly the best possible choice for spirit photography because it offers the greatest flexibility throughout the spectrum of photographic possibilities. This film is usually sold in either 24 or 36-exposure length.

The first thing you need to decide is what format you wish to use for the pictures. Will they be slides or prints? There are advantages for both. If you shoot slides or transparencies, as they are sometimes called, you can show them to your fellow researchers in a slide projector on a large screen. You can also make copies or prints from a slide as that acts as your negative. Ektachrome or slide film is usually expensive to buy but cheaper to develop as there is no Kodak paper to be printed on. Where print film is almost always less expensive to buy than it is to have it developed (for the most part).

Print film will produce a negative and copies can be made directly from the negatives but sometimes require the positive for color-matching qualities. This may be your best bet because the negative will be required if you do capture a ghostly image. Negatives would have to be examined for possible flaws and is the only true way of eliminating possible natural explanations.

What brand of film you use is a matter of choice, budget and reliability. Kodak, Fuji, Agfa and a number of other off-brands make some excellent films. However, I would recommend sticking to a well-known brand name and making absolutely sure the film is not out-of-date. All films have a date stamped on the box indicating when the film should be developed by. While some camera stores often have boxes and boxes of out-of-date film on their counters for sale at a substantially reduced price, I wouldn't buy it! It may be useless and you could be extremely disappointed if the film doesn't quite develop properly or at all. Especially if you know you have indeed captured something paranormal on film.

The next question is when and where do you intend to use the film. Will it be under low-light conditions? Indoors? Outdoors under bright sunlight? The speed of the film will be crucial to the use of the film. The smaller the number, i.e. ASA 64, the slower the film is and the longer the shutter will have to be left open for the film to gather the sufficient amount of light for proper exposure. However, the smaller the grain of the film, the better the picture quality will be and how large you can eventually blow-up that picture. Using very slow films allows you to make enlargements quite big without losing any picture quality but they are almost impossible to use indoor or at night.

If, however, you plan to use the film for shooting a cemetery at night or inside a house in subdued light, then you would need a faster film such as 400 ASA or above. These "fast" films gather light quicker and allow you to disable your flash and try time-exposures in a relatively short amount of time. A light meter might be helpful in this situation. The grain of the film is larger though, so enlargements will be limited as opposed to the slow films.

Should you use black and white or color? This depends again on the circumstances and the subject. If you are outdoors in a cemetery at night, perhaps black and white film would be sufficient as there will be somewhat of an absence of color. While indoors, you might prefer a color film. However, if you have more than one camera, you might wish to experiment with both black and white and color at the same time.

Choice of black and white film is, like choice in many fields of photography, far from an exact science. Fortunately, modern films are so good-natured, each type being able to cope adequately with a wide range of photographic possibilities, subject matter and lighting conditions, that as a result, inappropriate choice is rarely a disaster.

A fast film speed will, under given conditions, allow a higher shutter speed or smaller aperture to be used, which generally makes taking photographs easier. The choice should be related, where possible, to the type of photograph you are looking for.

Film speed has a close relationship to several photographic facts of life: graininess, latitude, contrast and resolving power.

The faster the film, the coarser the grain. However, as much as manufacturers improve film they cannot escape the physical fact that the size of the individual silver halide grains in the emulsion is smaller in slow films than in fast films. Both exposure and the degree and type of development influence the clumping together of these grains, which becomes evident in the finished product as the mottled effect of the graininess. Hence correct exposure and development can minimize the grain of a fast film, but it starts off with a built-in handicap against a slow film.

A film's ability to deliver an acceptable result when the exposure given is greater, or less than strictly correct, is widest with fast films. Slow films require accurate exposure and development to give the best result; fast films can tolerate underexposure or overexposure of several stops and still yield acceptable prints.

Though much influenced by development, contrast is also closely related to film speed, and the contrast of slow films builds up much more quickly than fast ones.

Resolving power is the ability to show fine detail and is higher in slow films than in fast ones. Measured scientifically, slow films resolve more lines per millimeter. Since the appearance of sharpness is enhanced by contrast, slow films have a much greater faculty for showing fine detail than fast films.

Fast films should not be selected for general use simply as an insurance policy against more careful technique, because of their good-natured latitude. Though modern fast films are good enough to produce adequate results in brilliant lighting or of even-toned subjects in flat lighting, for which they are least suited, they are best used to extend the photographer's shooting possibilities when the light is low but a high shutter speed is essential. Obviously they score highest for indoor conditions, photography in poor light and for use with very long-focus lenses with their restricted depth of field and relatively small maximum aperture.

Speeds of 400 ASA or above are usually given the title of fast films. Some films go as high as 3200 ASA, while you can often "push" film to increase it's light-gathering ability.

The nominal speed of a film is that which the manufacturer recommends for processing in a developer that gives optimum results. Processing in the more energetic developers, or in those which give finer grain, requires amendment either way to the film speed, and effectively extends the film's versatility. Thus the term "pushing" the film.

This apparent elasticity of film speed is employed with most fast films. An example might be: Ilford HP5, nominally rated at 400 ASA for seven minutes development can be rated at 800 ASA if developed for eight and a half minutes, 1600 ASA in the more energetic Microphen for 10 minutes and even 3200 ASA (giving an extra 3 stop exposure) for 15 minutes.

Inevitably, pushed negatives do not give optimum quality, and the technique really works best with subjects under flat lighting conditions. Most experienced photographers do not change because they have learned how to exploit the qualities and idiosyncrasies of their chosen film by long and patient trial and error. It is always best to simply buy a faster film rather than "pushing" slower film. You will immediately see a big difference in the finished product.

I'm not aware of the current prices for the very fast film. I suggest that you check with camera stores in your area to see what they would charge and, more importantly, if they will develop the film after it is shot. Many camera dealers and photographic laboratories farm out specialty film to more high-tech labs, which could take a great deal longer and cost even more. Plus you have to worry about even more "hands" dealing with your film. The less people that are involved with the development of your film, the better. Remember the old adage "Too many cooks spoil the broth."

If however, you decide to go with a color film, there are many things to think about. Let's discuss the basics of color film first.

The basic principle of color photography is that any color can be reproduced out of a mixture of only three basic "primary" colors - red, green and blue. White light, consisting of a combination of the three primary colors, can be separated into its components, but can itself be produced by combining red, green and blue lights. These three colors are therefore called the "additive primaries," and the production of multi-colored images by mixing them together is known as "additive synthesis."

Most practical color photography however employs the

method known as "subjective synthesis." Instead of beginning with three colored light sources, the subtractive method uses a single white light and creates various colors by filtering out the colors not contained in the desired color. The filters used in this method are colored yellow, magenta, and cyan and called the "subjective primaries," because each of these colors has the ability to block or subtract from the light one of the additive primaries. Yellow subtracts blue, magenta subtracts green, and cyan subtracts red.

The additive principle was used as the basis of the original demonstration of the possibility of color photography, conducted by James Clerk Maxwell in 1861. Three negatives were made of the subject - one taken through a red filter, one through a green filter and the last through a blue filter. From these, three positive transparencies were made. Using three projectors, each positive was projected through a filter of the same color as the one through which it had been taken: the red, green and blue image overlapped to create the first full color picture.

Actual color films consist of three layers of emulsion similar to the emulsion used in black and white film. Each layer is converted to a dye image at some stage of the processing, thus arriving at the same effect as three separate images. The top layer is sensitive to blue light, the second to green and the third to red - the same breakdown as black and white film. Light from the subject is recorded on the appropriate layer or layers of emulsion: red light, for example, will affect only the third layer, passing through the others, while yellow light, a combination of red and green, will be recorded on both the second the third layers. Several extra layers such as the acetate base are built into the structure of the film to hold it all together, but the basis of "tripack" film is in the three emulsion layers themselves.

A common myth about color photography is that it is an exact reproduction of an image. Since the photographic process involves slight distortion, colors of the result are hardly ever the same as the ones seen by the human eye at the moment of exposure. This is even more evident when one wants duplicates from the original negative. Most developers will ask that the positive also be included with the request so as to more accurately match the colors of the original positive to the requested duplicates.

. Nevertheless, color enables the photographer to record with a greater degree of accuracy than does black and white. A monochrome photograph is abstract at best because it leaves out an important visual element, color. However, the ultimate choice for spirit photography must remain with the photographer. The only exception would be Infrared film, where I highly recommend you use black and white rather then color for reasons I will explain in a bit.

My choice for fast color film would be Kodak 400 ASA. The grain is sufficiently small as to not make enlargements difficult and is fast enough to take under extremely low-light conditions. However, I do not rule out using faster film, if you can find it, or even pushing this film. Remember, when pushing film, you must inform the lab of the speed you shot the film at. In other words, if the film is rated 400 and you push it to 800, you must tell the lab technician that the film was pushed to 800 so that it will be developed properly. Otherwise, the pictures will be extremely dark and underexposed.

If you prefer to use black and white film then Tri-X 400 ASA film is ideal as it is slightly more sensitive to the Ultraviolet end of the spectrum and if used with Infrared, which is sensitive to the opposite end of the spectrum, you have a much wider area of both visible and invisible light covered for your experiment.

Now comes the tricky part of films in general, Infrared. Regular infrared photography can be defined as the technique of using a camera lens to focus an infrared image on a emulsion sensitized to infrared radiation in order to obtain a black-and-white negative record from which a positive print can be made with conventional photographic materials, or, if you prefer, what is commonly called, a "proof sheet." A proof sheet is simply the entire roll of pictures developed on an 8x10 sheet of photographic paper.

Infrared emulsions are sensitive to violet, blue and red light, as well as infrared. Therefore, Kodak recommends, a filter be placed over the lens to block out unwanted visible light radiation. A number 25 red is often recommended for general infrared photography because it limits the film to exposure by the red and infrared region of the spectrum, yet allows visual focus. This filter will absorb both blue and ultraviolet, which the film is sensitive to. A word of caution however, using a filter will again stop certain wavelengths and colors from striking the film. By doing so, you might be restricting the frequency in which a spirit operates. Therefore, I recommend not using any filter, but experimentation is something everyone should try.

The infrared end of the spectrum is from 700 to about 1200 nanometers. One nanometer equally a billionth of a meter. By using conventional cameras and techniques, reflected and transmitted infrared radiation can be imaged directly on film.

Some of the scientific applications include aerial photography, medicine, plant pathology, ecology, hydrology, geology and archeology, animal studies, pictorial photography and laboratory and laser photography. Aerial photography is primarily useful in enhancing the contrast of terrain, while medicinal uses include mapping venous patterns, outlining some subcutaneous tumors, and many plants under stress from disease, moisture deprivation or insects can be detected by infrared photography. This is extremely valuable in aerial forest and crop surveys for detection or plant disease. Color infrared 16mm film is often used and the reddish photographic rendition of healthy trees and plants grades into magenta, purple, green and brown as the loss of infrared reflectance progresses. And there are many, many other uses, including spirit photography, because we are now dealing with an area of the spectrum invisible to the human eye.

Infrared color photography began with the development of the film for aerial camouflage detection. Kodak Ektachrome Infrared film comes in 24 exposure rolls and is in a slide format. Unlike the usual color film, the three emulsion layers of this film are sensitized to green, red and infrared, rather than to blue, green and red. A yellow filter is used on the camera to withhold blue light to which these layers are also sensitive. When processed, a yellow positive image records in the green-sensitive layer, a positive magenta image appears in the red-sensitive layer, and a cyan positive image appears in the infrared-sensitive layer.

Color infrared used outdoors without any filter and under bright sunlight will turn the normal brightly-lit foliage bright red while trees and shrubs in the shadows and not illuminated by the sun appear blue or violet. Another problem with infrared film is since you cannot see the infrared light being reflected by your subject, it makes it impossible to properly focus the incoming IR light. Since no refractive-type lens can focus all wavelengths in the same plane, focusing a camera image for infrared involves consideration of the position of the image formed by infrared rays and possibly a shift from the visible focus.

This may sound complicated and usually I would simply tell the spirit photographer to ignore the above paragraph. However, to be completely correct and accurate there is a way to focus the IR light if you wish to experiment with that avenue of thought. Because infrared radiation is longer in wavelength than visible light, it will focus farther from the film plane, and thus, the visible should (or can) be adjusted. There are three principal ways to adjust for an infrared focus: (1) Focus visually and reset the focus ring on your camera so that the range determined visually is aligned with the IR focus mark usually present on most manual cameras (check your camera's owners manual for more information); (2) focus visually and move the entire camera (usually on a tripod for this method) away from the subject by 25% of the subject-to-lens distance; (3) focus visually and move the camera-back, or film plane (of a view camera), away from the lens by 25% of the lens-to-film distance.

Exact speed recommendations are not possible because the ratio of infrared to visible radiation is variable and because photoelectric meters are calibrated only for visible radiation. Therefore, make trial exposures to determine the proper exposure for photographs or make bracketing exposures. Bracketing your exposures is defined as a satisfactory way of guaranteeing a particular effect and is usually accomplished by taking three exposures , one at the calculated aperture, one a stop (or half-stop) above and one a stop (or half-stop) below the recommended setting.

For best definition, take all infrared pictures at the smallest lens opening that conditions permit. If large apertures must be used and the lens has no auxiliary focusing mark, establish a focusing correction by photographic focusing tests. A basis for trial is the extension of the lens by one quarter of a percent of the focal length of the lens. For example, a 200 mm lens would require a 0.50 mm extension.

Kodak High Speed infrared films may be used to obtain photographic records in some low light-level situations. Such conditions often prevail in law-enforcement surveillance and in audience reaction studies where some indication of the facial expressions is all that is necessary. A basic exposure of 1/30 second at f/1.8 is applicable in the following situations:

1) Visible tungsten radiation measures 0.5 to 1.0 footcandle incident at the subject.

2) The source coincident with (1) is replaced with clear ruby lamps of equal wattage to give a high infrared to visible radiation ratio.

3) One 250-watt GE Reflector Infrared Heat Lamp (250R40/10), or comparable, with ruby glass is used at a lamp-to-subject distance of approximately 40 feet.

4) The application of Sony Nightvision cameras, which project their own invisible IR light.

Try not to use a flash when you photograph since this will only tend to give you strange light reflections and flash bounce, which might be mistaken for a ghostly image. Plus, you are exposing the film to the entire spectrum of visible light. If you must use a flash, try placing a visually opaque filter transparency over the flash thereby only allowing IR light to be released from the flash unit and picked up by the film. For photography in the dark, a No. 87 or 87C Filter is recommended for filtering unwanted visible light from conventional light sources, such as electronic flash units. These types of filters would include the Kodak Wratten numbers 87, 87C and 88A. A deep, red-like the number 25 is very good as it permits the film to be exposed by both infrared and long-wavelength visible radiation. This is, again, another avenue to be explored.

Using the No. 25 filter with High Speed Infrared film, and exposing distant landscapes for 1/125 second at f/11 (or equivalent exposure) or nearby scenes for 1/30 at f/11, will result in scenes with black skies, brilliant white clouds and white foliage.

Using a yellow filter like the No. 15 with Ektachrome Infrared film, and bracketing the exposure around a film speed of 50 will result in blue-green skies, pinkish foliage, and slightly cyan skin tones...usually. Using a red filter like the No. 25 and again bracketing around a film speed of 50 will generally produce bright orange-red foliage, green skies and yellowish skin tones. A green filter like the No. 58 will frequently produce magenta foliage and deep blue skies and skin tones with a magenta cast. A blue filter like the No. 47 will often produce intense red foliage, red skin tones and white skies.

Black-and-white infrared film is relatively predictable here as far as effects are concerned, although you never know just how much infrared radiation is being reflected by your scene, and your light meter can't tell you.

Kodak infrared-sensitive films are packaged in equilibrium with 45% to 50% relative humidity. Storage of these films in high temperature or high humidity may produce undesirable changes in the film. For that reason, unexposed Kodak High Speed infrared film should be kept in a refrigerator or freezer at 13 degrees Centigrade or 55 degrees Fahrenheit (or colder) in the original sealed container. If the film is stored in a refrigerator, remove it one hour before opening the package to allow the film to warm to room temperature. This will prevent condensation of atmospheric moisture on the cold film or possible fogging of the film which, again, might not give you the desired results or even possibly ruin the film altogether. Keep exposed film cool and dry. This means avoid placing the camera in direct sunlight or a hot car for extended periods of time as the film is extremely sensitive to heat damage, which is IR light in itself.

Process the film as soon as possible after exposure to avoid undesirable changes in the latent image. If it is necessary to hold exposed but unprocessed film for several days, whether in or out of the camera, it should either be refrigerated below 40 degrees Fahrenheit. Obviously you don't want to place your entire camera into a deep freeze, so placing the camera in a cool and dark environment such as a basement or dark closet should be sufficient for a time. But the key thing here is, quick and prompt development of the exposed film.

Kodak Ektachrome Infrared Film requires more stringent storage conditions than those required for black-and-white infrared-sensitive films. Adverse storage conditions affect the three emulsion layers of Ektachrome infrared film to differing degrees, thus causing a change in color balance as well as in overall film speed and contrast. A loss of infrared sensitivity and a color balance shift toward cyan can typify film that has been stored under less than adequate conditions.

Kodak Ektachrome infrared films should be stored in a freezer at zero to 10 degrees Fahrenheit in the original sealed package. You must allow one and a half hours for the film to reach room temperature before use, as opposed to the hour needed for the black-and-white infrared film.

Exposed film should be processed immediately following exposure or returned to storage below 40 degrees Fahrenheit in the closed film container to minimize latent-image changes. A word of caution here, when purchasing either Ektachrome or High Speed infrared film from a camera store, be absolutely certain that the seller removes the product from a refrigerated unit of some kind. If the film has not be stored in such a manner, DON'T BUY IT! It probably means that the film has been heat-damaged in some way and is no longer fit for exposures.

Total darkness is necessary when handling both of these high-speed films, whether in camera loading and unloading or in processing. It is necessary, therefore, that camera, film holders, and darkroom be checked to determine that they are opaque to infrared radiation because any extraneous infrared energy is a potential source of fog. Changing bags, also, must be tested for "infrared opacity" before use in loading these films outdoors. Fog can be minimized by keeping loaded film holders and cameras in subdued light or in total darkness as much as possible. Heavy-duty aluminum foil and black Scotch Photographic Tape, 235, serve well as barriers to infrared radiation.

In lieu of a darkroom or changing bag, a pitch black closet, at night, will normally do quite nicely. Just be certain you know how to load film in your particular camera in the dark beforehand. You can practice this using ordinary film in a dark environment.

After the film has been exposed, you must also unload the film in total darkness. Again, I suggest doing this in the evening and in a dark closet or basement. A cave would be ideal if any were nearby. You will then put the exposed roll back in the original film canister and tape it completely shut with masking tape. Mark the canister properly for the camera store, including the type of film it is, speed you shot it at and making sure they understand it is infrared film. You might have to call several camera stores to see if they develop the film onsite or ship it out. Just because they sell the film, doesn't mean that they also develop it.

The reason I suggest going to such extremes as completely taping the canister shut is that the first thing most camera store employees will do when you present film to them for development is to remove the film from the original canister to properly log the type of film, etc. on their work-order envelopes. There is no surer way to destroy the film and expose it to unnecessary infrared and visible light then to remove it in this fashion. The plastic roll the film is contained in is not necessarily guaranteed to be light-tight.

I've had employees try to remove the film and had to tell them that the film was infrared. Some, not knowing what I meant, continued to try to remove the film until I had to explain to them that the film must be unloaded in total darkness or within a darkroom just prior to development.

The sensitivity of High Speed Infrared film is such that no safe light can be used during handling or processing as the beam of the light itself contains aspects of both visible and IR light to which the film is sensitive and can attribute to fogging. The film is processed in Process EA-5 or Process E-4 chemicals.

For additional technical information on Infrared film, I suggest you pick up Kodak Publications M-28 *Applied Infrared Photography,* N-1 *Medical Infrared Photography* and N-17 *Kodak Infrared Films.*

When you finally get the finished product from the camera labs, you can then begin to compare the IR film to the other "control" film that you were using to see if you have any anomalies on the film. Remember, if it shows up on both films, it was (most probably) something that was natural and nothing supernatural. However, if it only displays on the IR film and not the "control" film, then it's most likely something supernatural or, at least, paranormal.

Deciding which film to use when attempting spirit photography experiments, or actual investigations, is up to the individual investigator. You may wish to simply use a less technical and easier to handle film and by-pass IR for the moment. Down the line, you may wish to graduate up to IR as the results can be phenomenal and most interesting. Infrared film is very hard to handle, get processed and sometimes difficult to interpret and that alone turns many away from IR film. However, with the points mentioned in this chapter, I believe that everyone should at least try IR film at least once. You never know, you might like it!

Later, I will go into more technical information about how to analyze your results and tell the difference between natural and supernatural images, including some infrared flaws.

V. DIGITAL CAMERAS

The origins of digital cameras are intimately linked with the evolution of television in the 1940s and 50s, and the development of computer imaging by NASA in the 1960s. Before the advent of the video tape recorder (VTR), television images were optically displayed on monitors and then filmed by motion picture cameras. Because film and television technologies were essentially incompatible, Kinescopes or "kinnys" as they were called produced inferior images.

A breakthrough occurred in 1951 when Bing Crosby Laboratories introduced the VTR, a technology specifically designed to record television images. Television cameras convert light waves into electronic impulses, and the VTR records these impulses onto magnetic tape. Perfected in 1956 by the Ampex Corporation, video tape recording produced clear, crisp and nearly flawless images. The use of VTRs soon revolutionized the television industry.

The next great leap forward happened in the early 1960s as NASA geared up for the Apollo Lunar Exploration Program. As a precursor to landing humans on the moon, NASA sent out a series of probes to map the lunar surface. The Ranger missions relied on video cameras outfitted with transmitters that broadcast analog signals. These weak transmissions were plagued by interference from natural radio sources like the Sun. Conventional television receivers could not transform them into coherent images.

Researchers at NASA's Jet Propulsion Laboratory (JPL) in Pasadena, California developed ways to "clean" and enhance analog signals by processing them through computers. Signals were analyzed by a computer and converted into numeral or digital information. In this way, unwanted interference could be removed, while critical data could be enhanced. By the time of the Ranger 7 mission, JPL was producing crystal clear images of the moon's surface. The age of digital imaging had dawned.

Since that time, probes outfitted with digital imagers have explored the boundaries of our solar system. The orbiting Hubble telescope, a hybrid of optical and digital technology, maps the limits of the known universe. Here on earth, digital technologies gave rise to a host of medical imaging devices, from improved X-ray imaging in the late 1960s, to Magnetic Resonance Imaging (MRI) and Positron Emission Technology in the 1980s and 90s.

Today's digital cameras capture images electronically and convert them into digital data that can be stored and manipulated by a computer. Like conventional cameras, digital cameras have a lens, aperture, and shutter, but they don't use film.

When light passes through the lens it is focused on a photo-sensitive electronic chip called a charged coupling device (CCD). The CCD converts light impulses into electrical impulses (also called analog signal forms). The signals are fed into a microprocessor and transformed into digital information. The process is called *digitization.*

Although digital images do not yet match the quality of pictures produced on film, they represent an enormously flexible medium. Photographers are no longer limited by the physical properties of chemistry and optics. Computers outfitted with the appropriate software can augment and transform images in ways never before imagined.

Digital cameras come in several formats designed for the specialized needs of photographers. They range from inexpensive snapshot models to sophisticated scanner backs that fit on professional large format film cameras. Regardless of their size or sophistication, all digital cameras operate in much the same way.

All images we perceive are formed from optical light energy. Even digital images created within a computer are eventually converted into light energy that we can see. In order for a digital camera to store an optical image, it must be converted into digital information.

A digital camera gathers light energy through a lens, and focuses it on a CCD, which converts it into electrical impulses. These signals are fed into a microprocessor where they are sampled and transformed into digital information. This numerical data is then stored, and usually transferred later on to a computer where the image can be viewed and manipulated.

A black-and-white photograph is composed of a wide range of tonal variations. Like the spectrum of natural light it represents, the photo's tones are continuous and unbroken. By contrast, a black-and-white digital image consists of myriad points of light sampled from the light spectrum. A digital image's range of tone is determined by the camera's capacity to sample and store different light values.

After the CCD converts light into an electrical signal, it is sent to the image digitizer. The digitizer samples areas of light and shadow from across the image, breaking them into points or pixels. The pixels are next quantized - assigned digital brightness values. For black-and-white, this means placing the pixel on a numerical scale that ranges from pure white to pure black. In color imaging, the process includes scales for color resolution and chromatic intensity.

Each pixel is assigned an x, y coordinate that corresponds to its place and value in the optical image. The more pixels, the greater the image's range of tone. This quality is called *spatial density*, and is a vital component of image quality. How good a picture looks is also affected by *optical resolution* - meaning the camera's optics and electronics. Together, spatial density and optical resolution determine the image's *spatial resolution*, it's tonal spectrum and clarity of detail. In the end, the spatial resolution is decided by the camera's lesser most quality: spatial density or optical resolution.

If crisp, clear pictures are the result of spatial density, then a camera's digitizer should sample an image as broadly and often as possible. The digitizer's ability to do this results in the image's *spatial frequency*.

Imagine a picture of a palm tree on a sandy beach. The sky is blue with barely a cloud in the sky. The sand is golden, and covered here and there by white breakers. The ocean is an unbroken expanse of deep blue. The palm's dark forest greens are broken by shafts of filtered light. When the digitizer scans the image it will find the sky, beach and ocean fairly simple patterns of continuous tones. They vary little in brightness or color; one sampled point of light is pretty much the same as the next one. These areas have *low spatial frequency*. The digitizer doesn't need many samples to accurately read their tones.

The tree, however, with its deep shadows and brilliant highlights, presents a greater challenge. Bright tones and dark tones vary greatly from one pixel to the next. This rapid rate of tonal shifting is called *high spatial frequency*. In order to build an accurate representation, the digitizer needs many more samples than it does for a low frequency area.

After determining the area of highest spatial frequency, the digitizer calculates a sampling rate for the entire image. That speed is double the rate of the image's highest spatial frequency. In this way the digitizer captures all of the scene's subtle tonal nuance.

Of course, the camera's sampling rate is not infinite, especially in lower-priced models. It's ability to sample is limited by its number of pixels. Pixel density depends on the amount of capacitors on the CCD chip. This varies quite a bit between different makes and models of cameras. Generally, cameras are assigned spatial frequency rates that cover most situations photographers are likely to encounter.

They come in three varieties: consumer point-and-shoot, which produce low-resolution images (320x240 pixels), midrange, which produce average resolution images (640x480 and 1,024x768 pixels) and professional, which produce high resolution images (1,012x1,268 and 6,000x4,096). These come in two types: studio and field. Image resolution is an important consideration when buying a digital camera. Prices now range from just under $400 up to $29,000! The more control enhancements the camera is equipped with, the higher the price tag on the camera. The least expensive models have fixed settings for all controls (shutter speed, aperture and focus).

None of the point-and-shoot or midrange cameras will give you a 35mm film quality image. But, in most cases, the screen image quality runs from acceptable to very good in these types of cameras.

The apparent brightness of an object in the real world is quite different from its representation in a picture. Anyone who has ever gazed at the sun instinctively knows the difference between the actual object and a photograph of it. This may seem an academic distinction, but it is a key concept in digital imaging.

The sun, the moon, the trees and flowers - everything we see in our physical environment - possesses *radiant intensity*. They emit and reflect light energy. Paintings, photographs, and digital images, on the other hand, possess *luminous brightness*. Though they have radiant intensity, it is not the same intensity as the objects they represent. The sun shown on a television or movie screen does not have the radiant intensity of the actual celestial body. It is a representation.

In a digital photograph, each pixel has an assigned brightness value - a luminous brightness - that corresponds to a radiant intensity in the physical world. This value is determined by how many bits are in the quantizer.

A 3-bit quantizer, for example, can only render a scale of eight distinct tones ranging from pure white to pure black. If the camera took a picture of our beach scene, it would create a high contrast image with very few middle tones. This effect is called *brightness contouring,* and is similar to the phenomenon of posterization in conventional photography.

Brightness contouring has many pragmatic and creative applications where an image is ready to be manipulated in a computer. However, when capturing images with a camera, it's best to preserve as wide a tonal range as possible. Every bit added to a quantizer doubles its scales of tones. Most modern digital cameras are equipped with 8-bit quantizers capable of producing 256 different shades. Some professional quality cameras have quantizers that can render well over a thousand tones.

Making digital images in color requires an additional step. In black-and-white, the brightness resolution of a pixel is determined by one gray value. In color, that value has three components, one for each primary color, red, green or blue. This concept is called *trichromacy.*

Color digital cameras are outfitted with three different sensors, each one sensitive to a primary wave band of light. After an image is scanned and quantized, it is further broken down into color values. Each pixel is assigned three color values which represent qualities of red, green or blue. Color values are further distinguished by their hue saturation and brightness.

Suppose, for example, a photographer snaps an image of a pink balloon. The camera's red sensor is stimulated and the quanitzer assigns the pixels that hue. Next, a saturation value is determined. Deep red is a fully saturated color, while pink is much less saturated. It is relatively faded and much closer to the white extreme of the scale. Lastly, the brightness value determines the luminous intensity of the color. Is this a pink balloon drifting through the shade of a forest? Or does it float freely across a bright blue sky? These considerations will compose the saturation and intensity of the image.

Most digital images form within a blink of the camera's shutter. In that fragmentary instant, an image made of light is transformed into a stream of numerical data by a complex web of technologies. What's more, the image stored within the camera's memory chip is only the beginning. To be viewed and appreciated, the camera's data must be uploaded into a computer. Here, an imaginative photographer can alter and transform the image in almost any way desired. With the proper software, even the most mundane snapshot can evolve into a work of artistry.

The political, social and artistic ramifications of digital imaging technology are yet to be ascertained. One thing is certain: the way we create and perceive the fruits of human imagination will never be the same.

When you purchase your first digital camera, there are many factors to be considered. These "factors" will boost the price tag of the device. Some models have built in zoom lenses, which are limited to a zoom factor of about 3 times (approximately 38mm to 114mm). Some models will accept interchangeable lenses such as screw mount lenses used on video cameras. These options allow for close-up portrait and wide angle shots. Close-up lenses are also available for some models.

Most come with built-in flash. The higher-end models have a hot shoe for an attachable flash unit, allowing for better lighting options. Others have adjustable f stops (aperture settings). The lower the f stop setting, the better your image will be in low-light settings. Shutter speeds are also a consideration. Moving images require a faster shutter speed. 1/60 of a second is the lowest shutter speed for hand-held, stop-motion photography. Anything slower than 1/60th of a second requires a tripod. This holds true for 35mm photography as well.

The cameras vary in how many images they shoot, and how

they store them. How you will (in the studio or in the field) and what you will be shooting (still lives or race horses) will be a major factor when deciding what type of camera you will want to purchase.

Consumer and mid-range digital cameras now store anywhere between 7 and 82 images at a time (and this may and will change before this book goes to print). Flash RAM is the most popular way of storing images today. Its advantage is that it can store data even when there is no power going to the camera, and it can be used over and over again. The disadvantage is if you only have a little, you can only store a few images at a time.

PC Cards are an option some mid-range cameras are starting to use. This option allows you to switch out a card when one gets filled. The cards run from 2MB to 32MB storage capacity and enable you to keep shooting without downloading to a computer. The amount of images this media will store truly depends on the resolution you are shooting at the time. The higher the resolution of the saved image, the less you can store and vice versa. These cards are also reusable, but are a bit expensive. If you will be in the field shooting, this may be a better option for you.

Another option is that some digital cameras can also now store images on simple floppy discs and these discs can then be quickly inserted into your computer without having to download the same images through your camera. The disadvantage, of course, is the amount of images you can store on a 1.44MB floppy disc.

Be aware that most of the cameras available have at least two image quality settings (or may use interchangeable memory cards for extra storage space.) Images can be set to standard or high quality. Standard can run anywhere from 320x240 pixels to 640x480. High quality images can run from 480x240 to 1,024x768 pixels.

Some cameras have an instant viewer attached to the camera body, which allows you to view your shot instantly and decide to keep it or erase it and shoot again, without downloading it to your computer first, therefore saving storage space. If you decide to purchase a digital camera, I would highly recommend that you buy one with this feature! It will definitely pay for itself in possibly saving bad shots or, in the case of spirit photography, images that don't have anything suspect on them. This is, by far, the best and greatest feature of digital cameras: the ability to view your images right after they have been taken and make a field analysis of what you might have just captured. While it isn't always paranormal, you do have that option of an instant picture and the quality of the saved image is good also.

Most of the cameras come with software and connections for both Macintosh and Intel-based PC computers. They usually save in either JPG or TIFF format, or its downloading software will convert the image to your favorite format.

All of these great features might have everyone reading this book suddenly running out the nearest superstore to buy one of these electronic devices. However, there are definite downfalls to this digital technology especially under low-light conditions while using a flash. A number of people, in fact thousands, have picked up "orbs". What are orbs? Depending what website you visit, you'll get a different answer from spirits in orb formation, to dust particles, insects, light lag, mythical creatures, Egyptian gods (yes, I've heard this one recently) to what I truly believe the vast majority of these are: digital flaws.

Troy Taylor, President and Founder of the American Ghost Society headquartered in Alton, Illinois, began to conduct some research of his own on these "orbs" after having seen so many examples. A vast majority of them have been photographed with digital cameras under low-light conditions. So he thought there had to be some logical explanation.

I've known Troy for many years and I highly respect him not only as a friend but a tireless researcher who isn't prone to "holding back the truth" no matter how many toes he might step on in the process. And, according to some, including other websites, he's stepped on a lot. However, there's nothing wrong in telling someone that there orbs are nothing more than digital flaws in the current technology. In fact, you would be doing the field a great disservice if you didn't poke around for the truth and bring it into the light of reason.

On both Troy's website, and my website, there is a text file written by Troy detailing his research into the orb phenomena and digital cameras. I will let it be told by Troy in his own words:

"As I am sure that you have noticed in the pages that have come before, it has always been the philosophy of the American Ghost Society to try and rule out every natural explanation for a haunting before considering the idea that the cause of the phenomena might be a ghost. This is not because we are non-believers but because we are trying to provide authentic evidence of the paranormal. We do not make false claims about being experts but base our knowledge on our experiences, and not on what we want ghosts to be. We try to caution other ghost hunters about presenting questionable photos and materials, which do not serve as genuine evidence. We believe that such evidence should be approached with caution....that is to say that it is not real but unless there is other evidence to back it up, it cannot, and should not, be presented as ultimate proof of the paranormal.

"With those statements in mind, let's discuss why digital photography should not be used in paranormal research....

"There are many things that can go wrong when taking pictures from light refractions, which look like orbs or globes, to items that are caught in the camera flash and turn out looking really spooky in the developed print. It takes experience and practice to be able to realize what are faulty images and what are not. One of the keys is being able to analyze the photo and the negative and to be able to enlarge it and tell if the photo shows a natural image or a supernatural one.

"Which leads to my biggest problem with the new digital cameras that are becoming so popular in paranormal investigating....

"Now, before I tell you why I don't like digital cameras to be used in paranormal investigations, let me just say that I have nothing against the cameras themselves. I understand the benefits of them...the instant pictures, no wasted film and no developing costs. I understand the reasoning behind this. Digital cameras are saving ghost hunters a lot of money...but is this really a relevant reason to just accept what ever results come along?

"The idea of saving time and money are, of course, the positive points but unfortunately, the negative points to digital cameras outweigh the good ones....at least for their use in the paranormal field.

"Let me break down the objections that I have by first prefacing these comments by saying that not all ghost hunters with digital cameras are using them incorrectly. That is to say that they are using them as a secondary, back-up camera and not as the only type of camera used in the investigation. This is really the only way that a digital camera should be used.

"Unfortunately, not all ghost hunters are using the cameras correctly, which has led to some disastrous results on behalf of the credibility of paranormal investigating. Many ghost hunters are out snapping hundreds of digital photos at random, using nothing else in the investigation but the camera. It is these people who are presenting digital images as absolute proof of the paranormal who are making a mockery of spirit photography.

"No matter what some people claim, digital cameras CANNOT be used to capture irrefutable evidence of the paranormal and here are two reasons why:

"Some time back, I began to notice that digital cameras always seemed to capture images that were showing mostly globes or orbs and this made me curious. It was possible that many, even most, of these orbs could be genuine...it was only that it made me curious.

"So, I started talking to tech support people and engineers with the companies who made the cameras in question....including Sony, Canon and Hewlett-Packard. Now these folks had no idea that I was talking about ghost photos....all they knew was that I was taking photos in dark locations and these digital images were coming back with what looked like balls of light in them. Now these were photos that I was taking, not someone else. I had been experimenting with a digital camera and I had been suspicious of the results I was getting. All of the activity seemed to be just orbs.

As most of you know, this is the easiest type of photo to mistake for being authentic (outside of camera strap photos apparently) because of the various natural explanations behind them. I started to question the results, so I started doing some research.

"I had already noticed that, upon close examination, some of the alleged orbs appeared to be spots where the image had not filled in all the way in the photograph. This was precisely the explanation that was given to me by three different, unrelated companies. According to them, all three companies had been experiencing problems with their digital cameras when they were being used under low light conditions. It seemed that when the cameras were used in darkness or near darkness, the resulting image were plagued with spots that appeared white or light-colored where not all of the digital pixels had filled in.

"In this manner, the cameras were actually creating the orbs....which had no paranormal source at all.

"Remember, this was research that anyone could have done but I was soon to find out that some people just don't want to be confused with the facts! When I first made this new information public, I was attacked by various proponents of digital cameras who pretty much said that whatever opinions I had on the issue really didn't matter. I was just flat-out wrong! One of the few logical, and non-personal, arguments that were directed my way, said that the technicians at those three companies really knew nothing about taking ghost photos and would, of course, offer a skeptical view point about the images in question.

"Okay, now being a person with an open mind, I would concede that this is possible, perhaps even probable. But it still does not solve the biggest problem, nor does it address the fact that digital cameras will still NEVER offer proof of the supernatural.

"Here's why: To be able to analyze a photo and to be able to determine its authenticity, two things are needed..... a print of the photo and its negative. These are two things that digital cameras cannot provide.

"Last year, I sent a number of strange photos and negatives to

Kodak Laboratories, who authenticated them, and pronounced them genuine, but they had to have the photos and the negatives to do this. Both are required to prove that a photo is genuine because it must be possible to reproduce the photo from the negative and prove that no tampering or alterations have taken place.

"Obviously, this cannot be done with a digital camera. Also, as mentioned before, analysis of a photo begins with enlarging it to study the anomalous images. Have you ever tried to enlarge a digital photo very much? If you have, then you'll know that it becomes nothing but blurred images and pixels. Obviously, this makes it impossible to study it.

"Hopefully, you get what I am driving at here. Digital cameras certainly have their place and a number of benefits....I'm just not sure that they can really benefit the study of the paranormal. But who knows? Maybe changes will come in the future that will enhance digital and bring it up to the standards of the 35mm.

"But until that time, I suggest that you approach the digital photos that you see with an air of caution. Someone may be telling you they are the real thing.....and some of them might even be. As for the rest of them, well, I guess that's up to you to decide."

I couldn't have said it better myself and I applaud Troy for his research and feel his hurt due to the many attacks (by perpetrators who will remain nameless). The one non-personal attack that Troy mentioned though (in my way of thinking) still has no merit. It was from the person who said that the technicians knew nothing about taking photos of ghosts and would dismiss them anyway. Remember that Troy approached these people anonymously and without telling them that he was attempting to take pictures of ghosts. He only mentioned that he was taking photos in low-light or near dark conditions. Kodak has always been skeptical of spirit photographs and would probably simply dismiss them as some camera defect, development flaw or outright fraud. You must go outside the field of Kodak and other so-called camera experts to get an unbiased opinion.

I have seen hundreds of alleged orb photographs and haven't

found one single globe yet that has held up to intense scrutiny. The only thought I can leave you with as to using a digital camera is something that Troy commented on in his text file.....only use a digital camera as a back-up or secondary camera to an investigation or experiment. Perhaps even simultaneous pictures with both a digital camera and a Polaroid Instamatic. That way you will have two instant pictures of the same area, shot at almost the exact same second, give or take a couple.

And while you can indeed print out a digital image via a photo-quality printer and paper, it still isn't the same as a print from an original negative and cannot be reprinted for comparison purposes. The digital print would be identical, time and time again. So don't throw that expensive digital in the waste bin, it still can be used in some way during an investigation... just not as the only or primary camera.

VI. CAMCORDERS & OPTIONAL EQUIPMENT

The new wave of the future has always been the possibility of obtaining a spirit form on a camcorder, in other words, a moving image that covers more than one frame such as would be obtained from either a 35mm or digital camera. With the advent of the Sony Nightvision camcorders, ones that can literally "see in the dark", ghost hunters have a new tool in their attempts to capture that elusive image by some reviewable media.

The first commercial video recorder (VTR) was launched in the United States in 1956 for the television broadcasting industry. By the mid 1970s, models were developed for the home use, to record TV programs and to view rented video cassettes of commercial films.

Traditional video recording works in much the same way as audio tape recording does: the picture information is stored on a plastic tape with a magnetic coating. During recording, the tape is wound around a rotating drum inside the video recorder. As the tape winds its way through the machine and around the spinning drum, the video pictures are recorded on it. The audio signal accompanying the video signal is recorded as a separate track along the edge of the tape. With the new digital formats, the picture and sound information is recorded as "bits and bytes" and outputted as normal viewable pictures on your television screen.

Camcorder, compounded from "camera" and "recorder" became very popular in the 1980s in the VHS format. VHS is the world's largest most widely used system for recording and viewing videotapes. There are over six hundred million VHS recorders in use world wide. VHS technology was developed by Matsushita (Panasonic/JVC) in Japan in the mid 1970s and is still the most popular system worldwide. But the fact is that VHS is now stone-age technology. It's like using a gramophone record player for listening to music or, if anyone remembers, a Sinclair Spectrum for doing your word processing. They both work, but in terms of quality, they don't compare with their new digital formats now available.

Betamax was developed by Sony in Japan around the same time as VHS, had all the same features as VHS, and the picture quality was marginally superior. But marketing won the day for VHS.

For the last twenty years, the huge installed base of VHS recorders in homes around the globe has been the major obstacle inhibiting the commercial development of a new home video system. While Moore's law has seen computers advance at astonishing rates, the public has been stuck with VHS video. The advent of the DVD (Digital Versatile Disc) has signaled the end of the road for VHS as the only home viewing medium though.

The problem with VHS tapes, as far as camcorders go, is their size - even the smallest VHS camcorders are too big to bring on outings. In the late 1980s, as a solution to this problem, Sony developed Video 8, a small camcorder tape. The tape is about the same size as an audio cassette, the quality was good, and the format was widely used for home filming. A disadvantage of the video 8 system is that you cannot play the tapes back in your home video recorder. You have to plug your camcorder into the television to watch them.

A refinement to the video 8 is the Hi-8 system. The tapes look absolutely identical to ordinary video 8 tapes, but the picture quality is superior. The second home camcorder format was called VHS-C, and this was developed again by Matsushita. The tapes are slightly larger than Video 8 but their main advantage is that they can be popped into an adaptor and played back in your home video recorder. These later formats offered a clearer, sharper picture over the original formats, and, in some cases, allowed more hours of recording on a single tape than was previously allowed.

During the early 1980s manufacturers started using CCDs in security cameras. CCDs were quite low in resolution and many professional video applications still used tubes, as higher resolution images were only available thru the use of tubes. However, by the 1990s chip cameras replaced the aging CCD cameras. Chip cameras were potentially lighter (especially in high-quality cameras, where three tubes or three chips were used). They were also smaller and better in low light conditions and many had enabled a tendency toward more natural light shooting.

Tube cameras required period adjustment to keep scan accurate while chip cameras needed no such adjustment. Tube cameras were easily damaged by bright lights. Their Vidicom tubes experienced serious light lag problems and the real possibility of burning a permanent image into the tube when shooting into extremely bright conditions.

And now the future appears to be digital camcorders that can also double as a digital camera and record stills onto recordable media, which can then be later retrieved and downloaded into a computer. Do these digital camcorders run into the same problem as digital cameras in respect to capturing "false orbs" under low light conditions? There isn't sufficient research at present to say one way or another. That would be a good area for a reader to research!

The camcorder of choice for me would be a Sony Nightvision

camcorder and I've used them extensively at actual investigations both indoors or out. However, a real problem here is the very strong possibility of capturing something quite natural illuminated by the IR beam cast by the camera. What is this natural image? Bugs!

Even the smallest of bugs, mosquitoes, can be illuminated and be mistaken for orbs. I've seen quite a number of MPG or AVI files that have been sent through my website that display nothing more than insects whizzing around at night.

During the summer, when the insect population is at its highest, it's almost impossible to go out at night and not record an insect or moth flying through your field of vision. I've suggested in the past of using Yardguard or some insect fogger in advance of filming, but even that isn't a foolproof method.

The only foolproof method might be going out in the dead of winter when the insects have long ago been killed off by the frost and cold weather. However, that isn't so good on the equipment either as the camera and even the magnetic media can become fogged due to the difference in temperature and going in and out of doors.

During an investigation a couple of years ago at Mt. Thabor Cemetery in Crystal Lake, Illinois, we ran into that bug problem. The investigation was conducted on a steamy night in the summer and we were monitoring the nightvision cameras thru television monitors. There were thousands of little floating orbs being picked up. I immediately went to the camera in question and briefly illuminated the area with an ordinary flashlight. Sure enough, there were little tiny gnats, mosquitoes and other flying bugs within a few feet of the camera. Quite small, but large enough to be seen as "orbs" by the nightvision optics.

You must be absolutely sure that the area you are filming is free from insects, otherwise you will not know if what you film is natural or supernatural. And, the bottom line is, you will never be absolutely sure that the area is bug-free! Therefore, it's not a good idea to use a nightvision camera outside during warm weather months. Or, simply disregard the orbs and focus more on strange mists, shadows or figures, if you are so lucky! Any orb you pick up will most likely be a bug.

The thing that most disturbs me is when someone shows me a video that they shot under the above-mentioned conditions and becomes quite perturbed when I point out that what they most likely captured was only a bug. Some people become very hostile and downright defensive of their video. They claim that it cannot be a bug or insect under any circumstances. It's a very hard situation to be in, after all they did bring a video for me to examine and get my opinion on.

You must be able to take constructive criticism and perhaps even have your orb video or picture shot down as a natural phenomena, because most of the time, it is! I have even seen a videos shot with nightvision optics that showed a bright, fast-moving orb object in a darkened cemetery. It didn't take long for me to determine that what actually was being filmed was nothing more than someone's IR beam from their temperature gun that was captured and not a paranormal image. Remember anything that casts an IR beam can and will be picked up by the nightvision optics. Either take your readings before or after you start filming so that you don't photograph or film something quite natural.

The next chapter will actually begin to walk you through the picture-taking process with explicit dos and don'ts. However, before we begin that, let's look at some optional and recommended equipment that you might consider purchasing that can not only enhance the picture-taking process, but give your pictures much better quality as well.

<u>Optional Equipment</u>

I have already covered filters and their uses in a previous chapter, but you should probably pick up a few of the mentioned ones, especially for the use of infrared photography. The others, like a skylight filter is recommended simply to keep your expensive lens from becoming scratched while in the field. It is extremely less expensive to replace a skylight filter than it is to buy an entirely new lens. They can easily run into the hundreds of dollars.

Because filters are the cheapest of all accessories, and hundreds of types are available, they tend to be bought in unnecessary numbers. They can have as many abuses as uses, and until skill and knowledge have been acquired and tested, it is well to leave most, but not all, of them alone. Only if intelligently used can a filter improve a picture's quality.

Tripods are a must, especially under low-light conditions or when attempting long-time exposures, where the lens is manually opened up for a period of time. Unless your camera is firmly mounted on a steady tripod and good ground, your picture will be blurred or strange streaks of light will be captured by the unwanted movement of the camera in a hand-held mode.

Never attempt to take a picture without a tripod when the exposure setting goes below 1/60th of a second; the standard flash exposure setting on most cameras.

Tripods run from under twenty dollars to over a hundred or more, depending on the quality, durability and sometimes the name brand. If you are using more than one camera at a time, it's best to mount both of them on a single tripod using a dual-camera mount which can be purchased at most camera stores or retail department stores for a nominal fee. You will want your two cameras as close as possible so that they capture almost the exact same field of vision. Using two tripods is an option, however, it's extremely difficult to get two tripods close to one another without intertwining their legs. Even then, the images captured on the respective cameras is usually not a close enough view.

Tripods have the ability to elevate the cameras up and down, side to side and tilt up and down. Make sure the tripod you purchase has the ability to move the camera in every possible angle for easier manipulation of the view you wish to capture.

One of the most common causes of poor definition is "camera shake," the name given by photographers to their own frailty: in most cases it is the photographer who shakes. The effects of camera shake may not be obvious on contact prints, but enlargements will be ruined.

The slower the shutter speed, the greater the risk of camera shake, and anything slower than 1/250th of a second should be regarded as a potential risk. However, rather than restrict the flexibility of a camera that offers a full range of shutter speeds by never using speeds below 1/250th of a second, it is preferable to learn how to combat camera shake by holding and firing the camera correctly. In any case, fast shutter speeds will not solve the problem if the camera is handled badly. In other words, know your camera very well before you start!

The other critical factor affecting steadiness is the length of the lens used. Not only are long lenses heavier than normal ones, but they also tend to exaggerate the effects of the slightest movement. Much like using low-powered or high-powered binoculars or telescopes. The more the magnification, the steadier you will need to hold the device, else the field is hard to view as it's being bounced around. This is because the angle of view is so small that a minute change in the angle represents a large proportion of the whole picture: each movement is effectively magnified.

You can always rest the camera on a steady surface rather then use a tripod however you must be careful to gently press the shutter release otherwise the same problems will result. Even with a tripod, a shutter release should be used, and at very slow speeds it is essential. A pneumatic release works better than a cable release if the extension is to be longer than twelve inches. Cameras with electronically fired shutters need a special type of release.

You will absolutely need to have two releases, obviously, if you are using two cameras, positioning one in each hand and attempting to depress each at approximately the same time using the same shutter speeds and aperture openings for equal pictures. Using time exposures (holding the shutter opened manually) requires a cable release and you simply count the amount of seconds you wish to hold open the two lenses.

Experimenting will eventually make you a pro at how long a shutter can remain open before the film is over exposed. There are some devices that can help you determine this factor but they don't work very well under extremely low-light conditions.

A device to accurately measure the brightness of the available light is therefore advisable for black and white but essential for color film.

Light meters are used for this purpose. Some of the more sophisticated hand-held light meters, like the Lunasix, are as expensive as a modest camera. The needle gives a reading of the intensity of light, from which the required exposure can easily be calculated using the dials on top of the meter. A separate scale is used for special low-light readings.

The two materials traditionally used for this purpose are selenium and cadmium sulphide, but suitable new materials continue to be introduced all the time. An increasing number of cameras now include their own metering systems, the most sophisticated kind being the "through the lens" or "TTL" meters (nearly all using cadmium sulphide or one of the more recent materials), which monitor brightness of the actual image formed by the lens. Some are directly linked to the shutter and aperture controls to give fully automatic exposure. The TTL system is particularly well adapted to SLRs, allowing the photographer to carry out all the necessary adjustments (focusing, aperture and shutter speed) while looking through the viewfinder.

It is, however important to realize that light meters can be fooled. The reading given, regardless of type, depends exclusively on where it is pointed. If say, a large area of sky is included in the scene measured by the meter, the average brightness is likely to be considerably greater than that of the same scene without the sky. The meter will show a shorter exposure than required and the picture will be underexposed.

Designs have been produced that overcome such obvious pitfalls, but these always assume a typical set of conditions. If the actual conditions are not typical, the meter reading will have to be interpreted in order to achieve the desired result. The "center-weighted" system, for instance, assumes that the main subject is in the center of the frame, and that the main subject should be correctly exposed.

Many of the difficulties of obtaining technically excellent pictures have been simplified by the advent of reliable light meters, but it is still necessary to understand the equipment to make the best use of it.

The simplest way of taking a light reading is to point the meter at the subject, thus measuring the intensity of light reflected back to the camera, where the meter is held. One disadvantage of this method, however, is that the reading may be influenced by extreme bright or dark areas in the vicinity of the subject.

Using the diffuser over the cell of the light meter, the meter can be pointed away from the subject in the direction of the camera to measure the incident light. This method is more accurate, particularly with very dark or light subjects. A black cat, for example, would record gray if the exposure were based on a reflected light reading.

The principle of the selenium meter is that selenium produces a small but measurable current when exposed to light, with the size of the current proportional to the intensity of light. The meter circuit thus consists of selenium connected to a galvanometer, which measures electric current.

Cadmium sulphide, like the more recent substances in use, works on a different principle. It is a light-sensitive resistor whose resistance varies with the brightness of the light falling on it. A battery in series with the cell (unlike no battery with a selenium meter) supplies a steady voltage in the meter circuit. The galvanometer then measures the current in the circuit, which is proportional to the resistance of the cell. Because the cell need not be large to ensure high sensitivity, it is better suited to TTL metering systems. The special batteries used in the photo-resistor type continue to supply the same voltage throughout their working life, but will cease to function very suddenly.

Of course, you can eliminate the need to use light meters altogether if you simply use your electronic flash. However, you may not wish to light up the entire area for a brief but extremely bright fraction of a second. Flash glares and bounces off reflection surfaces are common instances of mistaken, accidental spirit images or suspect images.

The advantages of flash are proportionally high light output for the power consumed, the brief duration of the flash (eliminating the possibility of subject movement). The light from a flash is of constant power and duration and the exposure can only be controlled by the distance of the flash from the subject and the aperture used. Where possible it is preferable to bounce the light from a white wall or ceiling to produce a much softer effect, or to diffuse the flash with a white handkerchief, increasing the exposure as required. This will all but eliminate the possibility of direct flash bounce back or glare.

These are just some of the optional equipment pieces that you might want to pick up prior to conducting your own investigation or experimenting. I would definitely suggest a tripod as a mandatory rather than optional piece of equipment. Believe me, you will find some use for it down the road in a dark graveyard or in a house under low-light conditions.

VII. HOW TO PROPERLY ATTEMPT SPIRIT PHOTOGRAPHY

In the previous chapters you have learned about the very early attempts at spirit photography by some professional photographers who didn't intend to go out looking for spirits, but just happened to find them anyway. Eventually, they found a profit in faking spirits photographs and much doubt was cast on the whole field for generations to come. I have also explained the basics of camera operation, optional equipment to use and even suggested the type of films to better your chances of picking something up on the film. Cameras to avoid, or at least, not to use solo were also detailed in previous chapters. However, what you finally decide to use depends on your budget and how technical you wish get. I would suggest the simple basics at first, which could include an ordinary low-end 35mm and some kind of Instamatic camera. You can then, as your budget allows, upgrade to another 35mm and perhaps even add a digital camera.

How do you actually go about attempting to capture a ghost on film? Good question! It's still a matter of hit or miss and you will probably go through quite a lot of film, money and time before you get your first anomalous image. Or, you could get quite lucky and photograph something on one of your first outings. First you must choose your equipment and then someplace to experiment at.

If you are just starting out in the field, chances are you won't be called much by the general public to investigate a private house or business, at least until you are well established and known by the media. You might try a public haunted location as an alternative to a private residence. No matter where you live, there is probably some location not too far away that has a known haunted past. It could be a cemetery, church, murder site, accident site or some other place that is thought to be haunted.

Try going to your public library or historical society for information on what might be haunted in your neck of the woods. Most public libraries have circular files simply called "Ghosts", "Folklore" or "Psychic Phenomena", etc. that might be filled with newspaper clippings of well-known local sites. You might start with these. Also, libraries usually have quite a large selection of books on the subject that you could browse through.

If you are local to Chicago I would of course suggest picking up a copy of "Windy City Ghosts" or "Windy City Ghosts 2" as they have quite a number of haunted sites with the phenomena reported and exact addresses to most. There is also "Haunted Illinois" by Troy Taylor, "A Field Guide to Chicago Hauntings" by Jim Graczyk or "National Register of Haunted Locations" by Dennis William Hauck, which list hundreds of locations to choose from.

Always make sure where ever you decide to go that you either have permission by the owners, if it's private property, or that you don't trespass or go at night to places that might get you arrested. Forest preserves and cemeteries are good examples of places not to visit at night unless you have specific permission. Nothing places an unfavorable tag on the amateur ghost hunter than to get arrested for trespassing after hours.

Another way to experiment at this is by bringing along a cat or dog with you. Animals are extremely sensitive when it comes to spirits or psychic phenomena. They will often alert you to the possibility of something paranormal in a number of ways. Dogs might bark, growl or snarl at something unseen by you, but not to them. Dogs can hear sounds we cannot such as "dog whistles", which are high-frequency sound beyond the range of human ears. They can also pick up the slightest of scents that we cannot even be able to detect and they have that innate ability to see in the dark, perhaps even slightly shifted to the infrared area of the spectrum. Dogs might back out of or pull away from a certain area, fixate on an object, gravestone, etc., or even whine. These may indeed by signals for your team to try some photographs in the area to which the dog is reacting to.

Cats are similarly affected and sometimes hiss, spit, arch their backs or simply fixate or follow "something" with their eyes or head movement. While there may be totally natural explanations for their reactions, one cannot rule out the possibility of something paranormal being picked up by these animals. Young cats and dogs are the best. Try to get them out of their puppy and kitten stage perhaps in the 2-4 year range and don't attempt this with an older animal as they probably just don't care.

Yet another way to narrow the area down for your experimentation would be employ the use of a psychic, sensitive, medium or intuitive person that has either clairvoyant or telepathic abilities. I've used psychics in the past in investigations, some who have actually worked with local police in missing persons cases. It's trial by error with this method until you find one that works good with you and you begin to get some good results.

If you simply go to a site with your group and try random photographs, you are only hoping that something will appear on the finished film. I'll admit that this is how I began and I was using expensive infrared film. However, I guess I was just lucky as some of my first endeavors yielded some interesting photos.

Always go with a group when attempting spirit photographs for several reasons. First, there's safety in numbers especially at night and more people mean more hands and assistants to handle the equipment. A group of people might not miss a "visual" phenomena due to their numbers. It's also useful for your assistants to keep a photograph log sheet.

Prior to departure for your experimentation, you should put together on a word processor some kind of photographic log sheet. The sheet should include such items as camera, type of film, date, time, location, weather conditions and numbered from 1-36 (or as many pictures as your camera holds). As you take each picture, you then enter it into the log sheet. Describe why you took the picture (EMF meter, feeling, sound, etc.), which direction it was pointed at (use a compass) and any other information that would later be deemed useful when viewing the exposed image.

This is very important! Nothing is as frustrating as getting a bunch of pictures back and not remembering why you took them or perhaps even what you took. Diligent note-taking by your assistant will eliminate the guesswork and help in the later analysis of any image you might have photographed.

Never smoke nor allow anyone to smoke at any investigation or experiment. Cigarette smoke can and has been photographed as strange bluish-white fog, which could be mistaken as a ghostly image. If you decide to go out at night in the dead of winter, it's important to hold your breath while you snap a pictures as the steam from your mouth can be illuminated by your flash and also misinterpreted as a ghost.

Remove any camera or wrist strap from your cameras if you are using tripods or be sure to keep the camera strap around your neck if you are doing a hand-held picture. Otherwise, tape or otherwise securely fasten or affix the strap somewhere behind the lens of the camera. I have quite literally seen hundreds of hundreds of camera straps photographed by people. They often appear bright white, with serrated edges and are mistaken for alleged "vortexes".... whatever they are(?)

If you are using a non-TTL 35mm camera, be certain that nothing is in front of the lens as the view finder is often separate from the lens so it's not "What you see is, what you get". Most often people photograph their own finger or something in the foreground that wasn't seen thru the view finder.

Always know the exact weather conditions, most importantly Relative Humidity. An over-saturated environment can produce foggy or misty images, which are nothing more than your flash reflecting off the water droplets in the air. I'm not saying you can't experiment under those conditions, just beware of the possible circumstances. Experiment yourself by photographing your own breath, cigarette smoke, steam from either a humidifier or tea kettle or by even throwing baby powder into the air and flashing it. You'll be surprised at the results!

Decide if you plan on bringing a psychic person or an animal along and who will be documenting their reactions and feelings. If you don't know a psychic or don't have access to an animal, you could, of course, bring along some equipment that will again narrow the area to be photographed down to a much smaller site.

These are all things you should be aware of before arriving at the site to be photographed. However, after you've taken all of the above into consideration, then it's time to get down to business.

I am going to explain how "I" would go about experimenting at an alleged haunted location once I've done the research into the area and know the phenomena that has been experienced in the past.

You would need to bring along two 35mm SLR cameras, tripods, cable releases, an Instamatic camera, high pixel digital camera and some ghost hunting equipment including a good EMF meter, Raytec non-contact thermometer gun, air temperature and humidity gauge, compass, notebook, pens, pencils and logbook sheet.

One 35mm camera would be loaded with high-speed black-and-white infrared film while the other would have a fast black-and-white film like Tri-X. Both films would be exposed at 400 ASA and mounted on a single tripod using a dual camera mount.

Cable releases would complement both cameras. The Instamatic and Digital cameras would be used to "feel" the area along with the ghost hunting tools. Instamatic cameras are very sensitive to picking up anomalous images and unlike digital cameras, do not usually give false images. The reason for using a camera that gives an instant picture is obvious: let's you see what might be there instantly.

Sweeping an area with various ghost hunting tools is an excellent way to again narrow down that "area of experimentation". Tri-Field Natural EM meters are an excellent choice as they do not trigger natural energies but are more tuned to picking up supernatural fields. What you are primarily looking for are "moving" electromagnetic fields. Fields that make the device needles spike and which do not stay constant or static. Continuous readings are probably something caused by the environment.

Checking the Internet for the unusually high magnetic or radioactive readings is always a must!

Solar flares, sunspot activity, etc. can sometimes be picked up by devices, especially if you are using a Geiger counter. Before you jump to the conclusion that you are detecting something paranormal with your equipment, it's a good idea to pull the information off a site called "Today's Space Weather" at http://sec.noaa.gov/today.html. This site will give you detailed maps of a three day geophysical forecast in full color. It is extremely important and useful information that should be gathered prior to any full-fledged investigation or spirit photography experimentation.

Using your Tri-Field Meter, sweep the area to be photographed in a slow horizontal motion or, even better perhaps, place the device in the area stationary; as it's extremely sensitive to normal electromagnetic fields around us and fast motion just increases the chances of false readings.

If your budget doesn't allow a Tri-Field meter then a low cost Gauss meter can be employed. Just remember, the lower the cost, the less accurate the device will be. Ghosts can produce deviations in electromagnetic fields, which these devices will pick up. Once you find an unusually active area, you will need to try some instant photographs while your assistants begin to set up the 35mm cameras.

Depending on the lighting situations at the site you chose, you might have to use longer than normal shutter speeds and aperture openings. Placing the camera in a fully manual mode is recommended and disabling any flash units for the moment is ideal. Begin taking time exposures at five second intervals. In other words, each subsequent exposure should be five seconds longer than the prior one. Be sure to mark this information on the photographic log sheet so that when you see the finished product, you will be able to determine which setting works best for you under other similar conditions in your next experiment. If your location is completely dark, even a thirty second time exposure or longer will not be problem. A 400 speed film is sensitive but not overly so as 1000 or even 3200 film is. Overexposure should not be a concern here.

Another device you can use, and I recommend, are Raytek non-contact thermometer guns. I've seen photographs on the American Ghost Society website that clearly demonstrate how these can be used in conjunction with cameras. One picture in particular clearly shows a researcher pointing a Raytek upwards and an orb-like image hovering nearby. These devices should not be pointed however into the clear blue sky as they require something to reflect off of to obtain a reading. They are more a contact device then an ordinary thermometer. Using them in such a way will give the experimenter extremely low readings as the Raytek is searching for an object to register the temperature of. Some other brands even have a laser beam that can be placed directly on the area you wish to register. Be warned however that this beam of light will be photographed by your cameras. Don't mistake that for something paranormal.

Scanning the area with a device, that not only gives you an air temperature reading but the exact relative humidity is a must for the serious spirit photographer. You must know the humidity of the area you are attempting to photograph so that if you do get something that looks like a cloudy or misty fog, it could be something quite natural. Also the air temperature reading is better as it gives a more accurate and instant reading, which increases or decreases in tenths of a degree.

Cold spots are often signs that a spirit could be present as the theory is that a ghost uses the heat or faster moving molecules of air, which is energy it itself, to manifest perhaps in a physical form. By employing the faster moving molecules of air, it leaves in its wake, a cold spot, which is very local. Witnesses have claimed being able to step and out of a relatively small area of cold, which is sometimes quite intense.

Documenting an area with as much equipment and cameras as feasible is the best possible way of ruling out natural explanations and to keep debunkers and skeptics from punching holes into your research. Multiple cameras don't lie. However if you capture something on both cameras, it's most likely something that was already in the environment. If the infrared film shows something peculiar and not the Tri-X or control film, then perhaps you have an anomalous image that will require more examination.

That's one of the main reasons to use two cameras simultaneously. One camera can be tricked or show something abnormal, while two cameras complement themselves quite nicely. It's also a way to keep these debunkers and skeptics at bay. Rather than simply snapping pictures at random with single cameras, you will be using two or more cameras and perhaps some high-tech gear or some other means of feeling out the area to be photographed. However, even employing these strict and controlled methods will still invite those disbelievers to scoff at you and your photographic results. Don't let this deter you! There will always be skeptics and non-believers and most of them won't believe or agree with you or your findings unless the ghost comes right up and bites them on the.....well, you know what I mean.

There is some job for the debunker or skeptic though, as they will often point out possible natural explanations for photographic results. You need to be a bit skeptical at all times yourself but very open-minded. A closed mind is no surer turn-off of the paranormal than anything else that comes to mind.

Now when you believe you truly have captured "something" that might be a paranormal image is when the real fun begins. Because now you will have to attempt to analyze your film and rule out possible natural explanations yourself. Don't jump to the conclusion (like many websites that I've visited) that your picture is automatically an earthbound spirit. That is the fastest way to lose your credibility and believability in future endeavors. The next few chapters will take you through the analysis of your film, which does take some experience, and later, examples of both natural, faked and real spirit photographs will be discussed. I should hope after finishing the book that you will have a better understanding of what natural and supernatural photographs look like and how to tell the difference quickly and efficiently.

VIII. ANALYSIS OF YOUR SPIRIT OR NON-SPIRIT IMAGES

Just remember that most of the photographs that will come your way either through your own experimentation, from others via websites, email, etc. will have a natural explanation. It is, after all, extremely hard to capture a ghost or other anomalous image on film. It took me over two years before I had photographed what I believed (and still believe) to be unusual or paranormal; and remember the definition of paranormal is simply unknown and not supernatural or ghostly.

I have placed alleged spirit photographs into three main categories: Natural, Paranormal and Supernatural. Natural, of course, entails those pictures that can be explained away through natural sources such as bad film, double-exposure or even outright fraud; Paranormal, which indicates that a photo cannot be ruled out naturally nor is it categorized as Supernatural, it simply is unknown as to how the image in question appeared on the film; and Supernatural, the smallest and most profound category. This would include photos that appear to be of actual spirits or ghosts. Such examples would include the Brown Lady of Raynam Hall, the Tulip Staircase picture taken in Greenwich and others. However, your collection will probably include 80% Natural, 15% Paranormal and perhaps 5% or less of Supernatural. It's just that hard to actually photograph a spirit. But don't let those percentages stop you in your endeavors.

Let us assume you have either taken a questionable photograph or that someone has sent one to you for analysis. What do you need to conduct a proper analysis? First and foremost, you will require a copy of the picture and the negative. This is extremely important. However, if you wish to preview the picture prior to a more thorough examination, then a JPG or GIF file can be submitted via email before you request the negatives. This way you can see if you need to waste any more time on a very explainable image or request the negative for a more questionable and potentially remarkable image.

The exact conditions under which the photograph were taken are very important if the person who submitted the photo can remember. Items like weather conditions, humidity, temperature are necessary. You will need to know the type of camera used, film speed, was a flash used, etc. And perhaps most importantly, why was the picture taken in the first place. Was it an attempt to photograph a ghost? Was it a more benign reason such as a wedding, picnic, etc.? Is the area in question a known haunted place? And any other information that you can solicit from the picture-taker will be useful to a final analysis and explanation.

Some ordinary examples of accidental spirit photography can be caused by out of focus pictures. Out of focus pictures are caused when the lens is set at the wrong distance or when the subject is too close when using a fixed focus camera such as a 110 or 126 Instamatic. Problems caused by camera movement can look similar, except the entire picture is blurred. The solution here is to take care to hold the camera still during exposure and gently depress the shutter release. Camera movement during exposure is the greatest cause of blurry images.

Moving subjects require fast (high) shutter speeds. The faster the subject is moving, the higher the shutter speed necessary. Most fixed focus cameras are not good for moving subjects because they are set at a slow shutter speed. Most automatic 35mm cameras will take good action pictures outdoors in bright light or with flash. They will not take good action pictures indoors (or on very dull days) without flash because the shutter speed is programmed to slow down and to let in more light under these conditions. Most cameras with electronic flash (not flash bulbs) can take action pictures with flash and the further away you are from a moving subject, the easier it is to stop the action.

Serious lack of sharpness in the image is necessarily a mechanical rather than a chemical fault thru the development of the film. Camera shake is common: hand-held shots at shutter speeds lower than 1/30 second are usually regarded as impractical, and anything below 1/250 second requires care. Even with a tripod there is a danger of vibration from the mechanism of the camera itself, such as the retracting mirror of an SLR or a focal plane shutter. An image might be blurred simply because the shutter speed selected was too slow for a moving object. It is also possible that a blurred image may be caused by bad focusing. One of the elements of the lens may be out of alignment, in which case the lens needs repair, or the pressure plate at the back of the camera may be damaged in some way, which would mean that the film was not held flat during exposure.

During the enlargement process in a darkroom it is important to focus the image as accurately as possible, and stopping down before exposing the paper helps improve the depth of focus. The two most common causes of blurred images at this stage are enlarger vibration, and "popping" caused when the heat from the enlarger bulb makes the negative bulge during exposure, throwing it out of focus. To decide between blurred negative and print, check the grain or dust spots; if sharp, the negative is at fault.

Lens or skylight filters that aren't maintained properly, or become dirty, can yield weird images. A dirty lens, just like dirty eye glasses, can cause blurred pictures. Always check to see if the lens is clean. Wipe with a soft cloth or camera tissue, taking care not to scratch the lens or filter. Avoid touching the lens with your fingers. Open the back of the camera and clean with a soft brush. Make sure the back of the lens is clean on cameras where the back of the lens is visible. Dust, dirt or foreign objects on the lens or in the back of the camera will cause hazy spots or blurred pictures.

Spots on prints and negatives, whether dark or light, are usually caused by dust particles or other pieces of foreign matter. White specks on the negative suggest the presence of dust on the film before the exposure or before development, or grit floating in the washing water (these show up as black specks on the final print). White specks on the final print are usually caused by dirt on the negative during enlarging or, sometimes, by dirt on the printing paper surface. Fuzzy white spots on the print may be caused by dust that has gathered on the top surface of the enlarger condenser system. The remedy is meticulous attention to cleanliness at all stages of the operation.

If the spots are fairly large and round they may be caused by air bubbles trapped against the film or the paper during developing. Such spots appear white on the negative and black on the print if this occurred during processing of the film, and white on the print only if during the developing of the print. Insufficient agitation is usually the cause, and it can be avoided by tapping the development tank as soon as it is filled. These faults can usually be rectified by retouching the negative or the print.

Fairly large areas of staining on the negative, sometimes with increased emulsion density round the edges, are drying marks caused by persistent drops of water that dry slowly. This can sometimes be rectified by washing again and drying.

Light fogged film can be a big problem and there are many examples that exist today. Photographic film is very sensitive to light. Any unwanted light that strikes the film will cause damage to the pictures or ruin them completely. If a lot of light strikes the film it will be black and completely ruin the pictures. Opening the camera back will usually ruin some of the pictures and cause reddish streaks or blotches on others. This usually occurs during loading and unloading the film in bright and not subdued light. Always load your film in subdued light and total darkness for infrared.

A dropped or damaged cassette or disc may show light fog as a streak, or many streaks, on some of the pictures. Unwanted light striking the film evenly can cause off-color pictures. When this happens, usually a part of the film will be evenly fogged and part will be fogged in uneven streaks or lines. X-ray or heat can cause a similar problem. This can also be caused by a camera that is no longer light-tight. If you notice this happening on more than one roll of film, you might wish to purchase another camera or have the culprit camera repaired.

If a negative is fogged but the borders are clear, then the fogging could have been caused when the film was in the camera by light entering through damaged bellows or a faulty shutter, for example. If most fogging is at the edge of the negative, it is probably due to a badly-fitting camera back or a roll film being too loosely rewound on the spool, allowing light to leak in. The fogging of a negative over its whole area, including the borders, can be due to a large number of faults. These include excessive developing time; too high a developing temperature; developer exhausted or incorrectly mixed; unsafe darkroom light; light leaks in the camera, packing, darkroom or tank; stale film; and excessive exposure to air during processing. Developer that is too warm or exhausted may also give a dichroic fog that appears red by transmitted light and blue by reflected light.

This may also be caused by a fixing bath that is too warm or exhausted or contaminated by too much developer from previous prints, or by exposure of the negative to a strong light before completely fixed. The same faults also give rise to fogging on prints. Stray light from the enlarger during exposure may also fog prints, and in this case it can be diagnosed because the edges masked by the masking frame are left clear. Fogging along the edge of a print may be due to the paper having been stored in a damp or very warm room or close to a gas fire. Because film fog may also be caused by X-ray examination at airports, it is best to remove undeveloped film from luggage while traveling by air. Papers left lying near a safe light may be fogged overall and may show the outlines of those on top of them.

Scratches usually show up as a sharp line, or lines, going the length of a picture or pictures on a roll. The main causes are dirt or foreign matter in the camera back, a damaged cassette, rough rewinding of the film back into a 35mm cassette or rough handling of negatives brought in for reprints or enlargements.

Check to see if the scratches are on the negatives or only the prints. Little or nothing can be done if the scratches are on the negatives, but if the scratches are only on the prints it means that the prints were scratched during processing. Reprinting will correct the problem. If the scratches are on the negative, check the camera, if possible, for a rough spot or burr in the film path. If the scratches are on negatives brought in for reprints, caution the developers to handle the negatives by the edges only and very carefully to avoid scratches and further damage. Negatives do indeed scratch easily. While it is possible to scratch a roll of film during processing, it very rarely happens in modern photo-finishing labs. However, once scratched it is almost impossible to fully remove the scratches from a roll of film.

Scratches on prints may also be caused by careless handling of papers, scraping sheets against each other or handling them with sharp tongs.

Back winding or turning the rewind crank of a 35mm camera the wrong way when rewinding the film back into the canister can cause vertical marks on the film that resemble columns of light. Most 35mm cameras pull the film out of the cassette as the pictures are taken. After all of the pictures have been shot this film must be rewound back into the cassette. Some newer automatic cameras rewind the film automatically. Back winding cannot happen with these cameras. However, other 35mm cameras have a knob or crank to rewind the film after exposure. Usually a button or a switch must be pushed and the knob or crank turned in the direction of the arrow. 35mm film wound back into the cassette in the wrong direction causes the film to be bent or stressed causing unusual results when printed.

Objects obstructing the lens is all too common in photography but, it seems, especially in spirit photography. An object obstructing the lens causes a dark or black area on the print. This area always has a fuzzy outline, never sharp. However, when employing a flash, since the image is the closest object to the lens, it would be brightly illuminated. Vortexes or "white tornadoes" as they are sometimes called are nothing more then camera neck or wrist straps that are accidentally illuminated and then photographed. They almost always appear bright white, fuzzy with a serrated edge, just like a camera strap has. Look closely at the edge of a camera strap and you'll see what I mean. A camera case is the next most common obstruction after fingers, hands and straps.

This is very common in non-TTL viewfinder cameras that employ a separate viewfinder independent of the lens. In other words, in these cases, you would never know that your finger or camera strap is in front of the lens. The remedy of course is to keep fingers, hands, straps, cases, flash cords and other objects away from the lens. And, this may sound crazy, but be sure to remove your lens cap before taking pictures. I have yet to see a ghostly vortex or tornado that is not a camera strap.

Excessive exposure to X-rays or heat can ruin or degrade the quality of your pictures. Most USA airport systems are fairly safe (I've never come across a single problem to date), but if your pictures are very important or if you will be passing through many airports, it is safer to have your film hand inspected, or your camera, if it is already loaded. Airport systems in foreign countries often have higher doses of X-rays than USA airports. Be extra cautious when traveling overseas. And, in this day and age, don't take any pictures inside of an airport! They will confiscate your film for security purposes. I was once warned as I carried my camera around my neck.

Heat will degrade the quality of your pictures (especially

infrared), so store film and loaded cameras in a cool place. Avoid glove compartments, auto back window shelves and a closed car in the summer time. These places are very hot in warm weather and can severely damage the film rendering it almost unreadable. Modern films tolerate a lot of abuse, but keep them as cool as possible and process your pictures promptly. Remember that fast films (1000 ASA and above) are more easily damaged than slower films.

Flash reflections can degrade otherwise excellent pictures and are often mistaken for ghosts. Those places to especially avoid would be highly reflective surfaces such as polished wood, paneling, mirrors, metals and chrome. Avoid shooting directly into reflective surfaces but if not possible, then at least shoot at an angle or bounce the flash at an angle more than the horizontal angle of the subject.

The only real solution is to avoid getting this reflection in the first place by disabling the flash unit or by not using one at all. Even experienced professional photographers are fooled occasionally by chrome fixtures, curved eye glasses and mirrors. Once on the picture, a reflection is next to impossible to remove. Expensive retouching can help some situations, but usually is not satisfactory.

Sometimes shooting into the area of the sun can cause polygonal shapes on negatives. These dark shapes corresponding to the configuration of the diaphragm on the negative, often associated with dark streaks, are due to reflections of light between the lens elements. The only way to avoid this is to insure that the lens is shielded from direct sunlight. A lens extender shield is helpful here.

Overlapped or double-exposed pictures are caused in the camera when the film is not fully advanced or not at all. Sometimes the last picture on a 35mm roll will overlap the second to the last picture. This is caused by the fact that you have reached the end of the film and should not have taken the last picture. This usually occurs when more than the stated number of pictures are taken on a roll, i.e. 26 exposures on a 24 exposure roll. It also can happen, (but rarely), in a lab during printing.

When two totally different images appear on the one negative, the film has not been wound between exposures. With simple cameras this may be due to an oversight on the part of the photographer, but with sophisticated equipment the winding mechanism may be damaged. If the latter is the case, the more likely result is two images overlapping one another to some degree. If a moving element of a single image is recorded twice in a slightly different position it may be due to shutter bounce, when the shutter opens again after exposure.

A similar effect is when the flash is out of sync. Most cameras equipped with a focal plane shutter are only in flash sync at one shutter speed; other times it may be due to weak batteries. When faster shutter speeds are used, a portion of the picture is black. This portion can be almost all, half, or just a black strip (clear on the negative), depending on which shutter speed was used. The camera flash must go off exactly at the same time that the camera shutter is fully opened. When this happens, we say that the camera is in sync or synchronized.

Under-exposed flash pictures can also be caused by: improperly setting the film speed, standing beyond the limits of the flash or not allowing the flash to fully recharge, therefore, shooting the subject without the benefit of a flash.

Torn sprocket holes are usually caused by improper loading or rewinding of 35mm films. Many 35mm cameras have a button, lever or switch that must be used when rewinding the film back into the cassette. Failure to properly use the rewind button, lever or switch can cause the camera to damage the sprocket holes or in extreme cases tear the film in half. Torn sprocket holes can also occur when trying to take more exposures on a roll of 35mm film than stated. The film stops, but the sprocket in the camera keeps turning and tears the sprocket holes. Worse, you can pull the film completely out of the cassette.

I'm sure everyone has photographed the "Demon's eye" or red eye when attempting pictures of friends or relatives. Red eye happens on flash pictures when the subject is looking directly at the camera. It is actually a reflection of the flash in the subject's eyes.

There are many ways to avoid this problem. Move the flash farther away from the camera lens, make sure the subject is not looking directly into the camera, increasing the overall light in the room or, in modern cameras, using the red eye reduction feature. Another way would be bounce the flash off the wall or ceiling and not the subject itself.

Static electricity can cause various marks on your pictures. They can be spots, streaks or blotches. Modern films are designed to prevent static marks and in fact they are so good that they have almost been totally eliminated. Static marks can appear as yellow spots on print, sometimes connected by a yellowish line or lightning shaped streaks. This can occur during the rewinding of the film when the humidity is very low. This very low humidity situation occurs mostly in the winter time inside heated buildings.

Electrical discharges that crop up when handling unexposed film can lead to dark marks on the negative. These can take the form of uneven diffused bands along the film where fingers have wiped it or branching, lightning-like patterns due to sudden movements in a hot, dry atmosphere.

No exposure on the entire roll of film results in a completely blank roll of negatives and no prints. There can be many causes for this problem, including sending in an unused (new) roll in for processing, lens cap or obstruction over the lens during exposures, camera improperly loaded or camera malfunction such as shutter not operating or winding mechanism not working.

During my early years of photography, I sent in a roll of unused infrared film that was not properly loaded into the camera. In other words, as I was taking the pictures and manually advancing the film, I actually wasn't. If your 35mm has a manual film advance the best way to determine that the film is properly loaded is to thread the film through the take-up spindle, close the back, advance it a bit and then take up the slack. As you advance the film to number one, watch the take-up spindle to assure that it's moving. If it isn't, then the film isn't be taken up by the other spindle. Open the back, in subdued lighting, and try again.

A picture showing different image densities from one area to another means that either the negative or print has an uneven development. If it occurs on the negative it indicates that the developing tank has not had sufficient agitation or that there has not been enough developer in the tank. If it occurs on the print then the tray has not been agitated enough or the print has not been completely covered by the developer during developing. A gradual increase in density towards one end of the negative may indicate an uneven drying.

A yellowish-white negative is probably due to a deposit of sulphur from decomposing fixer and can be rectified by hardening in a 1% formalin solution and washing in 10% sodium sulphite solution at 100 degrees Fahrenheit. Greenish-black tones on prints are due to underdevelopment of chloride and bromide prints, over development of Kliewer-bromide prints, exhausted developer or excess potassium bromide in the developer. In these cases the print may be dyed.

Yellow or brown stains on the print may be due to insufficient agitation during fixing, exposure to white light before completion of fixing, insufficient rinsing between developing and fixing or exhausted fixer. Such a print may be bathed in the appropriate stain remover. Brown marks on hot glazed prints are often formed by insufficient fixing or washing and can sometimes be remedied by bleaching in a potassium permanganate bleacher and then redeveloping.

Green image tones may occur when stale paper is used or when the developer is exhausted and can be avoided by using a developer improver. A red, blue or green tinge on the negative support is the anti-halation backing, which should disappear during the processing. If it does not, it can be soaked in 5% sodium sulphite solution.

The network of fine cracks in the emulsion, known as reticulation, is due to washing the film at high temperatures or to using solutions of greatly differing temperatures.

The one constant that you've already probably noticed in almost every one of these explanations for suspect images is that you would have to examine the negative eventually to properly analyze the image in question. That's why digital cameras should be avoided as a solo piece of photographic equipment. Instamatic cameras and SX-70s produce a positive/negative. The positive print contains the emulsion to which the image was fixed by the shutter.

There are software programs on the market today ranging from the best and most expensive (Adobe Photoshop) to (Lview Pro and VuePrint Pro) shareware products that can be downloaded from the Internet for free. The manufacturers will allow you to use these products forever for free but suggest that you register them for a small fee. For that fee you normally get a better, more-upgraded version and periodic patches and updates on the software.

Using these software programs and a scanner, you can manipulate the image in a variety of ways including brightness, contrast, resizing, rotating, cropping, re-dimension plus changing the colors. Some allow you to actually unblur a blurry image by moving the whole image in the opposite direction of the movement. This can allow you to see the image in it's unblurred quality to an extent. VuePrint Pro will allow you to actually create a negative from a positive, which is most useful! And I always suggest scanning in the image at the highest quality that your scanner allows. This will allow you to zoom into certain areas of the picture with your software program without the picture beginning to pixel apart.

Of course, carefully examining the negative for potential chemical spills or development flaws is a must during a correct and thorough analysis. Plus, the negative allows you to reproduce the ghostly image again, if indeed it wasn't just a printing error on the original print. While it might be sometime before you feel you have acquired the expertise to properly analyze photographs, you can start right out and began taking the pictures first.

IX. PICTURES WITH NATURAL EXPLANATIONS

As mentioned previously, this category should be the largest as most alleged spirit photographs do indeed have natural and quite ordinary explanations. There are quite a number of so-called repeatable images that do crop up and I've seen hundreds of examples, for instance, of camera straps, humidity illuminated by flash, or the photographer's own breath on a cold day. The following examples were analyzed by the author personally and they are not paranormal at all. I guess it's beginning to sound like I don't believe that a ghost can be photographed. Not at all! Under the right circumstances and using the proper controls and cautions, it is very possible and probable that a spirit can be captured with film. The photographer just has to insure that all reasonable explanations have been addressed and safeguards are adhered to at all times.

With that in mind, let us look at some of the very early examples of spirit photography. Buguet and Mumler were the early masters in this field and some of the first alleged spirit photographs may indeed have been real. It was only later when they all decided that much money could be made by designing phony spirit photos and duping the public, which is exactly what they did.

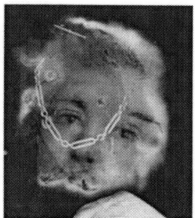

The Whiteford photograph and a close-up of the alleged spirit face.

A good example of early forgery came when the American, Edward Wyllie (1848-1911) photographed Mr. Robert Whiteford on October 7, 1909. A Scottish researcher into psychic phenomena, James Coates, sent locks of his hair and his wife's hair to Wyllie, who was living and working in Los Angeles. Wyllie used the locks of hair in spirit photographs, and one of the resulting spirits was recognized as Mrs. Coates' grandmother. This earned Wyllie an invitation to England, where his work was studied by Coates.

The photograph above shows Robert Whiteford, a photographer who, like Coates, lived in Rothesay, Scotland. It is one of two taken at Coates house by Wyllie in October of 1909. The entire procedure was conducted under the scrutiny of both Coates and Whiteford, who was described as a skeptic. Reproductions of the photographs, and the story of their production, are in Coates' book, *Photographing The Invisible,* published in 1911.

A close-up view of the ectoplasmic emanation shows blatant signs of brushwork and retouching. At one point in his career, Wyllie was accused of using phosphorescent drawings that would glow in the dark, apparently casting enough light on a developing negative to cause an "extra" to appear. Other spirit photographers palmed film negatives, which they surreptitiously placed over the negative. In this instance, however, it is difficult to guess at Wyllie's methodology because we don't know what the extra would have looked like without the intervention of the retoucher.

Moses A. Dow (1810-1886) founded *Waverley Magazine* in Boston in 1850. The magazine catered to amateur authors and reached a circulation of 50,000 copies before the Civil War. It continued to appear until 1908. Dow published the works of schoolgirls and other young writers; by one account he would print nearly anything that was offered to him for free. The tactic made him wealthy, because the friends and relatives of contributors would all purchase copies.

Mabel Warren was a young protege of Dow. She submitted her writing to him in 1862, when she was apparently fresh out of high school. He published her work and hired her as his assistant, a post she held until her death following a brief illness in July of 1870.

Dow was led into spiritualism by his housekeeper, who invited a medium to tea. Barely a week after Mabel's death, Dow felt his deceased assistant was communicating with him. In seance after seance, Dow received messages written mysteriously on slates or in ink on paper. Ultimately, Mabel's spirit directed Dow to Mumler's studio, where she promised to appear with a wreath of lilies on her head. Dow explains, *"The picture was small, but with the aid of a microscope it was magnified to the natural size of the human face, and in that face I saw the perfect image of my friend. I was both surprised and delighted and wrote to Mr. Mumler and told him I was perfectly satisfied, and gave him my true name."*

The picture in question was taken by Mumler circa 1871 and clearly shows the spirit of Mabel just to the left of Dow.

This image of an unidentified man with two spirits surrounding him, unlike the other examples, does not seem to show a celebrity or noted spiritualist. Perhaps the sitter is more typical of those who flocked to Mumler's galleries, seeking contact with deceased relatives or friends.

Members of photographic trade groups sought to condemn Mumler as a matter of professional pride and public service. The New York photographer Abraham Bogardus testified at Mumler's 1869 court hearing that he belonged to the National Photographic Association, which had among its goals "putting down any humbug we could discover." After the court dropped charges against Mumler, the Photographic Section of The American Institute passed a resolution "That the Photographic Section.....take the earliest opportunity to condemn all such methods of working upon the credulous and uninitiated."

The picture was an albumen print carte de visite, circa 1870.

Mumler sold copies of this next print through his ads in spiritualist publications, but provided no identification of the subject. The pattern of subtle mottling around the spirit child is typical of Mumler's works. It may have been a deliberate effort to hide seams or other evidence of subterfuge.

However Mumler achieved his effects, he was clever enough to fool two of America's leading photographers: James W. Black of Boston and Jeremiah Gurney of New York. According to Mumler's 1875 memoir, Black challenged Mumler to take his spirit photograph, and to allow him to examine the entire process. If a spirit form was produced, Black would pay Mumler fifty dollars. Mumler accepted the challenge and said when the spirit of a man appeared beside Black's figure on the negative, "Mr. B., watching with wonder-stricken eyes this development, exclaimed: 'My God! Is it possible?'"

Gurney, called to investigate Mumler by the New York *Sun*, later testified that he witnessed Mumler preparing and taking his portrait but did not discover any deception; *"in developing the negative,"* Gurney testified, *"I applied the chemicals myself, and upon the negative was a shadowy form."*

The picture was later identified as a Mrs. French of Boston circa 1868.

Boursnell claimed to have made spirit photographs as early as 1853, when extras appeared on portraits he was taking. The photographer, it was said, did not recognize the supernormal nature of these interlopers and blamed their appearance on improper cleaning of the glass used in the negative. One day, in a fit of anger, he dashed the negative to the floor, damning both the glass and the people who appeared on it. The extras did not return until 1886, when Boursnell became acquainted with spiritualism.

Because spirit photographers and mediums were subject to prosecution in Great Britain, Boursnell handed a printed slip to his patrons which denied the extras were spirits, instead it proclaimed they were shadows in the background. Critics charged that the same spirits appeared unchanged in different photographs, a sign of fakery. That revelation seems to have made no difference to Boursnell's supporters.

A hundred of Boursnell's spirit photographs were exhibited at the Psychological Society in London, and in 1903 the spiritualists of that city presented the photographer with a signed testimonial and a purse of gold.

The mount of this photograph is inscribed, "Taken by R. Boursnell in London on January 3, 1893. The spirit is an old family doctor who died around 1880."

Parkes was one of the first spirit photographers in Britain, beginning his work in 1872, the same year as Frederick Hudson. His earliest images were made in partnership with the proprietor of a restaurant, who served as medium. Following directions from the spirits, Parkes required that photographic plates be placed in his control in the darkroom before they were inserted in the camera (duh!), so they could be magnetized. If that aroused suspicions, Parkes tried to compensate by cutting a hole in his

darkroom wall so that his patrons could witness the processing of the negative.

The vertical line running through this photograph was caused by a break in the glass negative. Perhaps this was intended as a visual distraction, or served as evidence of paranormal vibrations.

Mrs. Collins' husband was an amateur photographer, who wrote a letter to the spiritualist journal *Human Nature* in which he hedges a little of the accuracy of this spirit likeness of his father. Judging by appearances alone, the late Mr. Collins could have served as the model for the Edvard Munch painting *The Scream*. It was taken in 1875.

Leymarie was the editor of *Revue Spirite* which circulated this next image and publicized Buguet's works. In 1875 a French court sentenced Buguet and Leymarie to a year in prison for fraud after a raid on the Buguet studio uncovered two shrouded dummies (the smaller of the two figures were used to represent children) and 299 photographs of heads, mounted on cardboard. Confronted with the evidence, Buguet confessed. But at the Spiritualist Congress in Brussels during September of 1875, he recanted, claiming that the dummies were only used by his employees when he was absent due to illness, and insisting that two-thirds of his ghost photographs were genuine.

The English medium and Angelic minister William Stainton Moses considered this one of the most important spirit photographs ever made.

Spirit photography, as you know, did attract many critics, prominent among them was P.T. Barnum, the famous showman. Barnum felt that the spirit photographers were taking advantage of those whose judgment was clouded by grief.

In April 1869 William Mumler was brought to trial for fraud. Barnum volunteered to testify against him, and to prepare to do so he asked Abraham Bogardus, a respectable photographer, to prepare the image here. In it, the spirit image of Abraham Lincoln can be seen floating behind Barnum's right shoulder. Barnum wanted to demonstrate that spirit photographs can be easily manufactured by any competent photographer.

At the trial Barnum made a point to differentiate between his own "humbugs" and those of the spirit photographers. He argued that despite his reputation for misleading the public, "I have never been in any humbug business where I did not give value for my money."

Mumler's studio was frequented by some of the most eminent people in the land and although in many of the pictures he produced undistinguishable "extras", on one occasion he produced a recognizable and astonishing psychic portrait of Abraham Lincoln.

A lady that was heavily veiled and wearing a black dress had given her name as "Mrs. Tydall" when she called unannounced at his studio and asked to be photographed. In his own words, "I requested her to be seated, went into my darkroom and coated a plate. When I came out I found her seated with a veil still over her face. The crepe veil was so thick it was impossible to distinguish a single feature of her face. I asked if she intended having her picture taken with her veil. She replied, 'When you are ready, I will remove it.' I said I was ready, upon which she removed the veil and the picture was taken." It was only when he saw the print that he realized that his sitter had been Mrs. Lincoln.

"The picture of Mr. Lincoln is an excellent one. He is seen standing behind her, with his hands resting on her shoulders, and looking down with a pleasant smile." It is by far, his most famous but probably fraudulent photograph.

This bizarre apparition of a cowled monk with a strange elongated white face was photographed by the vicar of Newby church in north Yorkshire, the Rev. K.F. Lord in the early 1960s. While there hasn't been much speculation about the authenticity of this image, it most likely is a fake.

The Episcopal clergyman who snapped the astonishing picture inside the church says his congregation has been at each other's throats ever since news of the photo was made public.

"About half of them think the image is of a genuine specter," says the Rev. Lark, "and the other half say it's a fraud." Rev. Lark claimed all he wanted to do was to take a picture of the church's altar. "The form was definitely not in the viewfinder of the camera," he stated. "The shrouded image appeared only after the photograph was developed."

Even two chemists Rev. Lark hired to run tests on the photo couldn't agree on an explanation for the eerie phenomenon. Consequently, the seemingly impossible presence of a ghost in the reverend's photo will likely remain a mystery, though at least one churchgoer says she knows exactly what's happening.

"This church has been haunted ever since I can remember," declared then 72-year-old Louella Sanderson, "I have often felt the presence of a spirit in the chapel during services."

A picture which depicts a robed figure, possibly Jesus himself, descending from the clouds has been widely publicized and distributed from Illinois, Texas, Virginia, New York and even Canada. The Canadian image was being circulated by nuns as

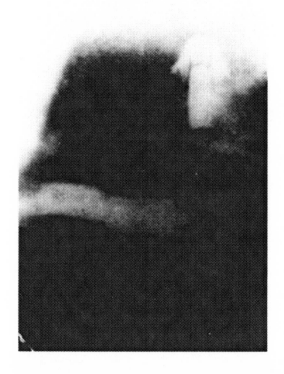

authentic. It seems to show a figure in white, his head obscured by the clouds, with outstretched arms and even a belt or robe around the waist, seeming to float out of a cloud bank into the clear blue sky. One version claims it was shot out of an airplane at 35,000 feet! This image is highly debatable but has never been proven to be an outright fraud or cloud illusion, although rumor has it that reproductions of the image were circulated in the 1970s by a religious organization in exchange for donations to the ministry.

One such Jesus image was allegedly taken by a teenager who claimed it is of a beautiful angel from heaven. Robin Aberzinski, then 16, took the photo while flying in a small private plane. She brought it to the attention of George Mason, a professional artist in Annapolis, Maryland.

"Robin took this picture while flying with a family friend over the Washington D.C. area," Mason said. "She intrigued me with her tale of photographing an angel. When she showed me the photos, I was just amazed.

"She told me she did the greatest double take of her life when she first spotted something outside the plane's window. Then she scrambled for her camera. She said this angel was wrapped in a flowing robe with a hood covering the head," Mason said.

Of course this story was told in the *Globe* , which is not exactly a reputable newspaper!

The exact same image was also claimed to have been photographed on October 14, 1975 by a Margie Brooks in rural Pennsylvania during a terrible storm. According to Hans Holzer's book *America's Restless Ghosts*: "There was a terrible flood and the sky was very dark. Suddenly Miss Brooks observed a figure in white in the sky and took that picture. Was it a way those from the other side wanted to reassure her of her safety?"

An ordinary television photographed (for what reason?) clearly shows a phantom hand reaching out from the top of the screen. Allegedly the television was unplugged and off at the time (how many people actually unplug and turn off their tv?).

This was taken on Christmas Eve, 1968 by a woman in southern Minnesota who snapped a picture of her husband assembling toys and inadvertently preserved an unscheduled broadcast on her unplugged television. The hand allegedly had appeared the year before, again at Christmas. There are many examples of floating heads and other weird images being photographed on television screens. I haven't decided in my own mind why people photograph their television sets. Are they trying to capture an image being played through the networks? When using a flash against a television that is turned on and running, the screen is usually blanked out due to the bright glare bounced off the reflective surface and outdoing the image being broadcast. Other pictures include images of what might be Elvis or Mr. Spock from *Star Trek*, to weird floating test images that seem to quite literally float right off the screen, continuing on the surface of a nearby wall. Use caution here as it is a highly reflective surface and unusual images are possible.

Now let's examine some later examples of accidental alleged spirit images. While analyzing photographs, I usually break the submitted pictures into categories: balls of light, streaks, misty formations, shadows and shapes, semi-transparent forms and full-fledged apparitions. I have examples of all. Some have been taken by myself while most were sent in through the Internet for analysis. These same categories will also apply when looking at possible "real" spirit images.

This first example is an Instamatic picture taken with a Polaroid Spectra 2 camera at Mt. Thabor Cemetery during an investigation sponsored by the Ghost Research Society. The picture was taken by me personally. Mt. Thabor Cemetery has had a history of producing some pretty astonishing pictures in the past including spectral forms, green mists, orbs and other floating images. Local researcher Stacy McArdle first introduced our group to the site and gave us the background history of the site.

A number of cameras were used that evening, however one suspect image was all that was captured. Near an obelisk-type monument I experimented with the Polaroid and within a minute we got our answer. A nicely formed orb appeared near the gravestone. I would consider this picture more paranormal than either natural or supernatural because it's quite hard to determine if this is nothing more than a bug or insect that was photographed. It's quite possible that an insect was very close to the lens of the camera and when photographed became diffused and out of focus causing the orb-like image.

Now, let us examine another orb-like photograph. This one was submitted for analysis and, at first glance, there are many, many orbs in the photograph, plus what looks like a cloudy image to the extreme right. It doesn't take a rocket scientist here to quickly look at the conditions under which the film was exposed. It's in the dead of winter with snow on the ground and either blowing or falling precipitation in the air. A flash was used that only further illuminated the snow. They are not paranormal orbs or ghosts and furthermore, the mist or cloudy image to the right of the picture (more than likely) is nothing more than the steam or heated breath exuding from the mouth of the picture-taker.

I have seen many outdoor pictures taken under similar conditions that display almost identical results. This can also occur when photographing under high humidity conditions when minuscule water droplets can be illuminated by the flash and photographed. The picture-taker will always state that they didn't see anything when the photograph was taken. Of course, they didn't because some of these water droplets are quite small. Other similar examples could be rain droplets, mist or virga which is nothing more than rain evaporating before hitting the ground.

It is very important to note the weather conditions on all outside experiments or investigations that you conduct. Using temperature guns, thermometers and hygrometers that register relative humidity are important to later ruling out natural explanations. Sling psychrometers that employ the web bulb, dry bulb way of telling you humidity content can also be used. There is nothing more frustrating than receiving a photograph from someone with insufficient information regarding weather conditions or having them guess, or try to recall from memory, conditions that could have happened years ago. It's just not a reliable way of obtaining the pertinent and necessary information you will need to conduct a proper analysis.

However, more orbs are photographed with digital cameras under low-light conditions than with anything else. As explained earlier, they are nothing more than digital flaws where the pixels failed to fully construct that portion of the picture. The following photograph was taken in the wine cellar of the Alton, Illinois McPike Mansion in 2001 in total darkness! You couldn't see your hand in front of your face. The conditions inside the cellar were cool and damp with a relatively high humidity. It was taken by Ghost Research Society lifetime member, Donna Boonstra with a newer digital camera. Until the flaws are worked out, digital photography should take a backseat to the more foolproof 35mm cameras of today.

There are at least two distinct orbs, one over the head of fellow researcher Howard E. Hight and another in the ceiling over researcher Monty McClennan. We had returned after a more thorough investigation the previous night to conduct some additional tests and with the help of owner Sharyn Luedke, we attempted to invite the spirits to make an appearance. Needless to say we weren't disappointed. This picture, not withstanding, we heard on two separate occasions the distinct sounds of footsteps coming down the stairs into the basement and then the metal door leading to the wine cellar actually creak as though someone was attempting entry. Both times the area was thoroughly searched with no natural explanation for the cause. It was videotaped at the time, and you can clearly hear the sounds on the audio portion of the video tape and see the concern in Sharyn's voice as she calls out to see who was there. The mansion is currently condemned and the owners are attempting to save it from the wrecking ball. If you would like to help assist them in fund-raising or donations you can call Sharyn Luedke at 618-462-3348.

Mists and fogs happen for similar reasons. Usually it is due to temperature fluctuations or other natural explanations such as someone smoking a cigarette too close to the camera. This is, now, next to orbs, the most often captured alleged paranormal image that I've received for analysis. A lot of the times, it's something very simple and explanation; others are more harder to determine the cause or causes.

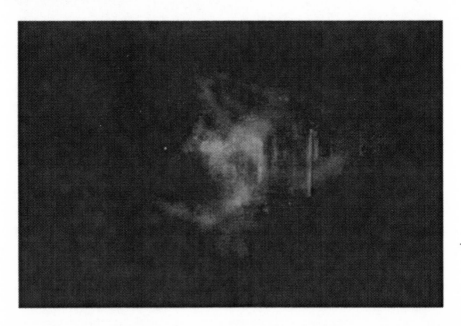

In this photograph, again taken outdoors and at night with a flash, a 35mm camera was used and the picture was taken around 11:35 PM on December 24th. It was quite cold outdoors with approximately 4-6 inches of snow on the ground at the time. A multitude of explanations are possible including temperature, humidity, etc., but I believe this to be just the steam coming out of the picture-takers mouth. Usually unfiltered cigarette smoke, in other words the smoke given off by the simple burning of the cigarette and not the expelled smoke, is quite easy to differentiate as it's usually thick-looking and very blue-grayish in color and is often in swirls and not a thick mass. However, the most important thing to remember when taking photographs is to be aware of your surroundings and what the people nearby are doing. Never allow anyone to smoke while taking photographs and hold your breath if it is extremely cold outside.

Vortexes, "white tornadoes" or swirls are becoming more common to see everyday. If you visit ghostly websites, you will probably see some of these examples. They almost always look identical because the object being photographed is indeed identical in all, namely the camera or wrist strap of a camera. This happens more often when you are tilting the camera 90 degrees to the left or right. Try to envision your camera and the neck strap. It's normally attached both to the left and right of the camera lens. If you don't keep the neck strap around your neck, it will dangle below the camera for the most part. As you tilt the camera downwards, it's possible to have the strap in your picture. More often, when the camera is tilted to the left or right for a vertical rather than a horizontal picture, the strap is more likely to weave in and out of the picture. If the picture is taken without a flash it will often be a dark image as in this first image which clearly not only shows a camera strap but even the neck support attached to the strap!

Most of the camera strap photographs that are sent to me are the whitish, vortex-like ones taken at night with a flash. In this case, the camera strap will appear to be bright white, somewhat fuzzy, with a serrated edge and trailing out of the frame in one direction or another. The reason the image is bright white is simple; it's the closest object to not only the camera but the flash unit as well. When the picture is taken, the strap may be swaying in one direction or another, the flash unit will strike the closest object to it, illuminating more so than any other image in the area. Henceforth, the white, fuzzy, out-of-focus, serrated edged strap has now become a ghostly image or vortex. I would suggest you try deliberately to photograph your camera or wrist strap and compare that image to ones later sent to you for analysis. You've be pleasantly surprised to see the very distinct similarities between the two. They should appear almost identical!

Such is the case in the next three examples (I could have showed you more than a hundred). The first one appears to run diagonally from upper right to lower left and has the semi-transparency seen in all such examples. Why? Remember the strap is most likely in motion, that's why it's not seen as the picture is taken, and because no solid portion of the strap is in frame for more than the exposure time, it appears to be translucent in appearance.

The next image is a textbook example of a vertical shot taken around Christmas time of someone's Christmas tree. The camera was most likely rotated 90 degrees to the left causing the camera strap affixed to the right of the lens to droop over the lens when the shutter was released.

Henceforth, a ghost of Christmas present?! No, it's totally explainable. Again notice the serrated edges and semi-transparency in this image. Those are constants that will be easy to spot in other examples you will come across.

The last example shows a family pet being photographed with a ghostly image nearby. Now since the camera was pointed downwards in this picture, what was photographed was most likely a wrist strap, which is much smaller than a neck strap and is only affixed to one side of the camera; either the left or right of the lens. The camera used was a

zoom(?) camera and brand was unsure by the picture-taker. That's the email I received in the sender's own words, which were, as you can see, very much frustrating and lacking greatly in information about camera, film, etc.

But since the explanation sticks out like a sore thumb, no further information was really needed to make a correct analysis in this instance.

The rule of thumb here is to either remove the neck or wrist strap from your cameras prior to experimentation or investigations, keeping them firmly around either your neck or wrist or making certain they are, at all times, behind the camera and therefore the lens. While accidents do happen to non-professionals and professionals alike, they should not allowed to happen while attempting spirit photographs. It's hard enough to produce an authentic image without accidentally snapping something perfectly explainable.

Another problem arises when using film that is either too slow for the action you are photographing or shutter speeds which are too slow for the movements you are taking. This results in objects or people appearing as see-thru or semitransparent. The first image was taken in the U.S. Capitol Building in Washington D.C. Obviously, nothing out of the ordinary was seen while taking the picture, however when the taker viewed this frame later, he thought he had photographed a ghost. A semitransparent figure of a man is seen in dead center of the frame moving from left to right. He is dressed in gray pants and a gray shirt and his head can quite literally be seen through! This is caused by the movement not being able to be frozen by either the shutter speed used or film, which was probably too slow as well.

This second image is located on my website and was shot by my webmaster Matt Hucke at Bachelor's Grove Cemetery. It is a deliberate attempt at producing a ghostly image to show you just how easy it can be. This image was made by placing a camera on a tripod with an exposure setting of ten

seconds. The subject, wearing a long black coat, stood in front of the camera for about three seconds, then ran out of the frame, resulting in a semitransparent image. I have actually seen some deliberate attempts at spirit photography that were sent to me for analysis. It was, as in this image, quite easy to determine the cause for the picture. However, some quite legitimate pictures of a similar nature turn out to be genuine. Caution and care should be exercised in analyzing semitransparent forms as they could turn out to be the real thing!

I've probably seen more alleged spirit pictures taken at Bachelor's Grove Cemetery in the south suburbs of Chicago than anywhere else. It attracts both the amateur and professional photographer and ghost hunter alike. This next image taken at Bachelor's Grove Cemetery facing west into the setting sun is nothing more than lens reflection of the sun striking the hexagonal-shaped lens. Remember you have glass and mirrors within your camera's interior and even though you might not be shooting a highly reflective surface, care must be used in photographing into extremely bright light or sunny conditions. If you can see it in your camera viewfinder, then it will appear on the finished product. It's really quite easy to obtain an image like this one, so just use common sense when photographing into the setting sun or brightly lit conditions.

Sometimes a more pronounced effect can occur as in this next example. Multiple hexagonal-shaped images are possible when the camera is pointed in precisely the exact position. This effect is always quite easy to diagnose and the solution to future such pictures is possible only by abiding by simple good judgment for camera placement or by using a lens shade to cowl the actual lens from the unwanted bright light. The hexagonal-shaped images are usually the same color as the object you are photographing. Yellow or orange are the most often photographed colors.

A similar image is often caused by loading or unloading your film in bright light not subdued as recommended by the film companies. This will always cause a reddish blur or haze on either the beginning or end of the film depending if you were loading or unloading it. Sometimes it can appear on more than a few pictures. Always load and unload the film in subdued and not direct lighting conditions. This will prevent this reddish blur from appearing on your film.

Other conditions of light leakage into your camera will often leave behind either vertical or horizontal lines on some pictures. This occurs mostly on pictures that are allowed to be framed up and ready to shoot but might remain in this ready mode for several days. The light leaking from a camera that isn't light-tight can cause a vertical or horizontal streak of light that usually is bluish-white. The longer the picture is framed-up, the brighter the streak will be. If this happens to your pictures on more than one roll of film, it is wise to have the camera examined by a professional to find the source of the leak or, better yet, just buy or use another camera.

Just remember that there are more natural than supernatural explanations for most alleged spirit images that you will come across in your work, analysis or experimentation. Don't jump to conclusions! Don't be afraid to possibly offend someone who has submitted what they believe to be a genuine image when it's not.

The surest way to get an undesirable reputation is to post perfectly explainable images on your website or in a book which aren't. I've seen hundreds and hundreds of examples on such websites that are nothing more than digital flawed orbs and vortexes and mists and fogs that are probably caused by the difference of temperature. When I approached the webmaster or owner of the site to give my opinion, I was simply told that I didn't know what I was talking about and they often deleted my message from their guest book. Only trying to be helpful sometimes can often backfire on you, so be cautious and choose your wording carefully when attempting to offer alternative explanations for alleged spirit photographs. I've gotten to the point where I have to laugh a bit when I see some of the allegedly authentic spirit photographs on someone's site but now I keep my mouth shut and say nothing. The real professional or seasoned spirit photographer will be able to tell the difference immediately. Eventually through trial and error and coming into contact with a number of alleged spirit photographs, you become better equipped to tell the difference almost immediately as well.

When someone brings a photograph to you for analysis, it's sometimes better to just simply shake your head in agreement but not commit to real or natural than to try to be confrontational with them. People really become quite offended when you "burst their bubble" regarding their spirit photograph. If you feel this may be the case in a particular situation, remain neutral and only offer your opinion if they specifically ask for it. I usually say something like, "Oh, that's interesting!" or "Pretty unusual!" These phrases make it sound to the client that you are showing an interest without committing yourself one way or another. It's a simple matter of public relations but still showing an honest interest.

People very often do not remember the exact circumstances under which the picture was taken, which is essential for a proper analysis. Others will swear their camera does not have a camera strap, no one was smoking, the temperature outside was cold but not cold enough to see your breath, it wasn't humid or hadn't just rained or even that they used a flash even though a most definite flash glare can be seen in the picture. You must use your expertise and rational judgment while analyzing all photographs. Once you've seen enough of them, like I have, you will be able to sometimes make a good call within a few minutes of seeing the photograph.

However, when you finally do come across the image that

doesn't fall into the above mentioned categories, seems highly unusual and you just feel that there is more here than meets the eye....you may have finally stumbled across your first *real* ghostly image. The image can be something paranormal or unexplainable or perhaps, just perhaps, a real ghost captured on film. The latter is extremely hard to come across, but not impossible. To verify either one, extreme documentation is required, including the circumstances involved with the picture-taking, positive and negative and the equipment used such as camera and film. The next chapter will deal with those images I believe to be authentic examples of ghosts, taken both by professional camera persons and the amateur alike. Let us now cross that hard to reach threshold and delve into real ghost images.

X. EXAMPLES OF REAL SPIRIT PHOTOGRAPHS

This is what you have been trying to obtain all along.... indisputable proof of ghosts and henceforth, life after death. You have been looking for hard evidence that will even send the hardcore skeptic into a head-scratching frenzy and pictures that have been subjected to extreme analysis procedures and have upheld that procedure with flying colors. You search for images where all the necessary documentation was there for the analysis and negatives as well as positive prints were available for scrutiny. They are photographs that do not fall into any explainable category and the film and camera have been thoroughly checked out.

It's these pictures that I've strived to see for over 20 years. I will predict that you will eventually either photograph or come across such a picture yourself at some point. Maybe it will be sooner than later, it's really hard to say. The circumstances were real; the people taking the picture were believable and, in your opinion, not playing a prank or trying to fake a spirit image; and, it just simply looks like a ghost or phantom. Sometimes it will just look too good to be true. Often, this is true but who's to say for sure?

Let me lead you through some of the most famous spirit images of the past before showing you some more contemporary pictures that are just as startling. The following images have never been exposed as frauds and they were often submitted by people who either didn't believe in ghosts or weren't trying to photograph them in the first place. In other words, ordinary photographs taken sometimes by ordinary people under ordinary conditions when something extraordinary was photographed.

One of the most amazing images to date, and one that has no natural explanation, is the very famous Brown Lady of Raynham Hall in Norfolk, England in 1936. Many reports involved a figure moving quietly down the staircase, along one of the corridors, and in and out of one of the first-floor bedrooms. The figure being a clear and distinct one dressed in a gown of brown satin and yellow trimmings and a ruff around the throat. The features were quite clearly defined but the eyes are sometimes dark hollows and her cheeks have been described as unnaturally white.

The ancient house that stood there was renovated by the Townshends when they purchased the property in the first half of the nineteenth century and one of the well-attested sightings of the famous Brown Lady occurred when Captain Frederick Marryat (1792-1848) came to stay. The son of a distinguished politician, he was a British naval captain and famous author of such books as *Mr. Midshipman Easy* (1836), *Peter Simple* (1834) and *Masterman Ready* (1841). This knowledgeable and honest seaman claimed to have encountered the Brown Lady during a visit to Raynham Hall in 1835, when he was among the guests of Lord and Lady Charles Townshend.

There had been numerous reports of phenomena, including a phantom carriage, right up until the time the Dowager Marchioness Townshend agreed to have some photographers visit the locale in 1936. She was interested in the subject of ghosts and quite fascinated by the resulting photograph. It was arranged that two top professional photographers, Captain Provand, art director of a Piccadilly firm of Court photographers, and his assistant Indre Shira, would visit the Hall and take photographs for *Country Life* magazine. On the morning of September 19,1936, they arrived and took a large number of photographs of the house and grounds and then, at about 4 PM, they came to the oak staircase. Indre Shira described what happened next in *Country Life* dated December 26, 1936.

"Captain Provand took one photograph of it (the staircase) while I flashed the light. He was focusing again for another exposure; I was standing by his side just behind the camera with the flashlight pistol in my hand, looking directly up the staircase.

"All at once I detected an ethereal, veiled form coming slowly down the stairs. Rather excitedly I called out sharply: 'Quick! Quick! There's something! Are you ready?' 'Yes' the photographer replied, and removed the cap from the lens. I pressed the trigger of the flashlight pistol. After the flash, and on closing the shutter, Captain Provand removed the focusing cloth from his head and, turning to me, said: 'What's all the excitement about?'

"I directed his attention to the staircase and explained that I had distinctly seen a figure there - transparent so that the steps were visible through the ethereal form, but nevertheless very definite and to me perfectly real. He laughed and said I must have imagined I had seen a ghost - for there was nothing now to be seen. It may be of interest to record that the flash from the Sasha bulb, which in this instance was used, is equivalent, I understand, to a speed of one-fiftieth part of a second.

"After securing several other pictures, we decided to pack up and return to Town. Nearly all the way back we were arguing about the possibility of obtaining a genuine ghost photograph. Captain Provand laid down the law most emphatically by assuring me that as a Court photographer of nearly thirty years' standing, it was quite impossible to obtain an authentic ghost photograph - unless, possibly, in a seance room and in that connection he had had no experience.

"I have neither his technical skill nor long years of practical experience as a portraitist, neither am I interested in psychic phenomena; but I maintained that the form of a very refined influence was so real to my eyes that it must have been caught at that psychological moment by the lens of the camera.....

"When the negatives of Raynham Hall were developed, I stood beside Captain Provand in the dark-room. One after the other they were placed in the developer. Suddenly Captain Provand exclaimed: 'Good Lord! There's something on the staircase negative, after all!' I took one glance, called to him 'Hold it' and dashed downstairs to the chemist, Mr. Benjamin Jones, manager of Blake, Sandford and Blake, whose premises were immediately underneath our studio. I invited Mr. Jones to come upstairs to our dark-room. He came, and saw the negative just as it had been taken from the developer and placed in the adjoining hypo bath. Afterwards, he declared that, had he had not seen for himself the negative being fixed, he would not have believed in the genuineness of the picture. Incidentally, Mr. Jones has had considerable experiences as an amateur photographer in developing his own plates and films.

"Mr. Jones, Captain Provand and I vouch for the fact that the negative has not been retouched in any way. It has been examined critically by a number of experts. No one can account for the appearance of the ghostly figure; but it is there clear enough...."

This photograph has stood the test of time and experts and is still considered today to be unique and a true example of a ghost. One of the earliest examples, I might add that was not faked or retouched and the people involved are of impeccable stature.

The next example is equally amazing! The famous case of the ghost of the Tulip Staircase in Greenwich, England has also proved to be one that is hard to dismiss, even though some experts have done so in the past without much success. Remember there's always someone, somewhere, who won't believe in the authenticity of a photograph and will try to debunk it. It's easier to try to disprove a photograph then it is to prove.

While on a visit to London in 1966 the Rev. and Mrs. R.W.

Hardy from White Rock, British Columbia, Canada, visited Greenwich and photographed the Tulip Staircase in the Queen's House. When the transparency was developed, after their return to Canada, a shrouded figure is clearly visible clutching the stairway railing. Some even say two figures! (There are always attendants on duty in the vicinity of the staircase to ensure that no one attempted to pass the barrier and climb up, and also to safeguard the many valuable paintings housed there.)

The original photograph and transparency eventually made its way into the hands of the prestigious Ghost Club in England founded in 1862. It was then submitted to Kodak and other experts, who all agreed that there was no trickery, or manipulation, or double-exposure, or any duplicity as far as the transparency was concerned; the only logical explanation they could offer was that there must have been someone on the stairs. I doubt that the attendants on duty that day the Hardy's visited the staircase would have allowed anyone access to the staircase and surely not dressed in monks garb!

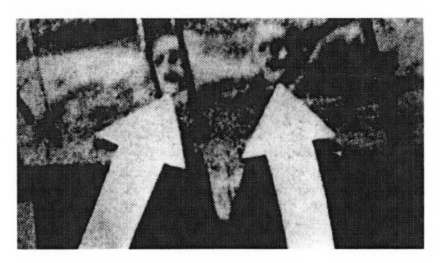

The case of the *SS Watertown* is yet another example of what many believe to be a true ghost photograph. The story, as recounted by the eminent and long-time director of the American

Psychical Institute, Dr. Hereward Carrington, and as detailed in the house magazine of the shipping company, told of the tanker, *SS Watertown*, making its way through the Pacific Ocean in December 1924. Seaman James Courtney and Michael Meehan were assigned to clean out a cargo tank. While doing this task they were overcome by gas fumes and died before help could reach them. Following the tradition of the sea their bodies were committed to the ocean on December 4th.

The following day, just before dusk, the entire ship was in uproar when the heads of the two dead seamen were clearly seen on board ship and, later, in the sea. Thereafter the ghost faces were frequently seen and understandably became the chief topic of conversation in both officers' and seamen's quarters. A snapshot was taken and the camera, with film intact and untouched inside, was handed to Captain Keith Tracy for safekeeping. No other camera was aboard the vessel, so no substitution was possible.

On reaching port in New Orleans the Captain handed the camera over to officials of the Cities Services Company and they sent it directly to their New York office, where the film was developed and printed by a commercial photographer, and there were the heads of Courtney and Meehan, exactly as they had been seen on board ship! As Carrington himself described it, the two 'spirit extras' were 'remarkably clear' on the photograph - and recognized by people who knew the men in life.

On a return journey. and in the event the two phantom heads were seen again, the Captain inserted the film into the camera and took six exposures. When the ship again docked the Captain took the camera containing the film, which had not left his possession, to Mr. James Patton, an officer of the company, who in turn took it with him to New York where it was developed by a commercial photographer.

The first five exposures showed no abnormality but on the sixth the heads of the two seamen were clear and sharp. Neither the shipping company, who at one time exhibited an enlarged copy of the photograph in the lobby of their New York office, nor

Hereward Carrington, nor anyone else, has ever explained the picture - the original of which sadly must have disappeared. The negative was checked for evidence of fakery by the Burns Detective Agency, and the circumstances in which it had been taken were attested to by the *Watertown's* captain and the assistant engineer.

Miss Sybil Corbet photographed the interior of Combermere Abbey, Cheshire, England, in December, 1891. When her photograph of the library was developed, it showed the figure of a man sitting in an armchair. The figure seems not to have any legs, but was recognized as that of Lord Combermere who had been in the habit of using that particular chair. But at the time, his body was being buried some four miles away.

She developed the plate herself and photographed the library using her camera on a steady tripod. No ghostly image was either seen or felt on the day of her visit. The image only later appeared on the developed plate.

During a trip to Australia in 1959, Rev. R.S. Blance went to Corroboree Rock, a well known aboriginal ritual site near Alice Springs. To his surprise he found he had also caught a strangely garbed figure to the right of the clearing that only appeared on the developed film, Blance said. One of the first full-color images of a ghost which appears to be a robed figure with something on his head and his arms have been risen to his face as if in prayer or perhaps drinking something. (see photo on following page)

Haunted houses provide excellent venues for taking supernatural and psychic photographs and old churches and ancient ruins are also good sites for such photographic experiments. A Mr. Neville Davies of Waltham, photographed by his wife beside King Richard's Well in Bosworth, was to be nothing more than a scenic shot taken at a well known historic site. The larger than life extra image of a man in mediaeval clothing wearing the white rose

of York on his breast is clearly seen between Davies and the well. Bosworth Field was the scene of the battle in which King Richard III was killed. Again, nothing was seen at the time as is the case in most spirit photographs.

Mrs. Mabel Chinnery, of Ipswich, Suffolk, England, visited her mother's grave on March 22, 1959, to take a few photographs, and used up the film snapping her husband alone in the car or so she thought. A friend, seeing the photos later, pointed out the image of Mrs. Chinnery's mother sitting in the back seat, to the Chinnery's astonishment. Although when she took the photograph her husband was indeed alone in the car, the photograph clearly shows her late mother sitting in the back seat in which she usually sat when they had taken her out for a drive.

This next photograph depicts the interior of Eastry Church, Kent, England and was photographed by a bank manager in September of 1956. There were only three other people in the church at the time, all behind the camera! This image clearly represents a semi-transparent figure of a priest with white collar around his

neck, dressed in black, perhaps holding onto a cane in front of him. There has been no speculation as to who the figure might be however the facial features are very recognizable.

The previous pictures were highly publicized and I'm sure that most of you have probably come across some or all of them in your readings of the paranormal and spirit photography. The following photographs are ones of a more contemporary nature either taken by myself, members of the Ghost Research Society or submitted for analysis through my website. Some of them are truly amazing and one of a kind. If you come across something similar in your work, consider yourself very lucky and fortunate. Most of these ghost photographs are well defined or show what

appear to be figures in them. I have personally analyzed them and believe that they are genuine examples of spirit photography.

The first ghostly image is of a girl standing on the porch of her house once located in downtown Chicago, on the north side. The house is no longer standing but a Jewel Food store now occupies the property. I wonder if anything unusual has been reported there in the past?

The paranormal image was taken with an older Polaroid Land

camera and clearly visible on the stairs and surrounding area is a strange smoke-like fogginess, which is semi-transparent in places and more visually opaque in others. It is sharply 'cut off' on the extreme right of the fog as though someone simply cut it with a knife. Strands of filaments of the fog seem to be exuding from the stomach region of the girl on the stairs suggesting that perhaps he is the source of the phenomena.

Is this what psychic researchers call ectoplasm? Living organic substances exuded from the bodies of material mixed with an odd mixture of fibrous hairs, dust particles, etc. Psychics and spiritualists would call this stomach area a "charka". Charka comes from a Sanskrit word meaning "wheel", symbolizing the seven major centers of the body. The image leans more toward being categorized a "psychic" photograph rather than a "spirit" photograph. A psychic photograph is defined as an image created, caused or made to happen by either the photographer or the subject of the photograph through either "Thoughtography" or the ESP of the people near to where the picture was taken; much as Ted Serios was able to impress images on unexposed photographic plates and films through the power of his own mind.

Ted Serios, self-described as an "unemployed Chicago bellhop", came to the notice of Dr. Jule Eisenbud early in 1964. Serios had an ability he would demonstrate to anyone who took an interest. He could project mental images onto photographic film, sometimes with the lens cap still on, and sometimes with no lens at all on the camera. His talent was unpredictable and seemed to depend on Serios working himself up, then glaring at the camera through a small cardboard tube he called his 'gizmo'. The gizmos were constantly examined by investigators and never contained anything suspicious. Dr. Eisenbud was intrigued enough to spend more than a year studying Ted and his results.

On one occasion Ted produced an image identified as an old livery-stable in Chicago that was located a few days later and photographed with Ted posing outside. In Ted's picture the window and door are elongated and appear bricked up; the texture of the wall differs from that of the real building; and attempts to trace a wall-poster that matched the one to the left of the door failed. Eisenbud concluded that Ted had not photographed the real building, but somehow obtained an image that contained distorted elements from his memory or imagination.

There was no way to identify the origin of some of Ted's photos, like one shot apparently showing a Russian Vostok spacecraft, while others clearly seem to be images seen in magazines, or films, etc., filtered through Ted's mind. The Royal Canadian Mounted Police identified one photo as one of their Air Division hangers but Ted had left his mark in the misspelling of 'Cainadian'. Once, trying to picture the Hilton hotel in Denver, Colorado, Ted obtained an image of the Chicago Hilton instead.

He seemed to work best when boozed up a bit and matched sealed target images placed in envelopes prior to any experimentation and known to only two researchers. Again and again he would match the target image. In a moment of bravado, Ted suggested that he could even impress images into a television camera. Many strange images were indeed received instantly. If the images weren't coming from the mind of Ted Serios, where were they coming from?

During his study of Ted Serios, Dr. Jule Eisenbud learned of the effects produced by brothers Richard and Fred Veilleux and their families, of Waterville, Maine. The brothers began experiments with a Ouija board in 1966 through which they received instructions about when and where to take pictures.

Among their first paranormal effects was a photo of Carol, Fred's daughter, in Pine Grove cemetery, in June 1968, showing her surrounded by inexplicable fogging.

In April 1970, the Ouija board told the brothers to focus upon the east wall of the smallest room in their father's apartment. The result was a strange scene of a chariot. At the same sitting Biblical quotations were given that related to the chariot.

A phantom face appeared after the brothers were told, in June 1968, to point the camera at the east wall of Fred's kitchen and wait two minutes before taking the picture. They could not identify the portrait until two years later when they visited Denver, Colorado, while working with Dr. Eisenbud. They found a copy of a historical magazine, *The West*, which contained an almost identical face, that of a long dead sheriff named Scott White.

For several years, Dr. Berthold Schwarz, a practicing psychiatrist with a keen interest in UFO phenomena, closely studied Mrs. Stella Lansing, a Massachusetts housewife, whose psychic abilities unfolded after a series of UFO sightings and a close encounter. Stella was often impelled to start filming by chills or hunches, and produced over 500 regular 8 and Super 8 color frames on each reel revealing phantom faces, geometrically arranged marks and other curious effects, including artifacts that look like classic UFOs.

In 1973 Stella visited her employer, Mr. C. and his family, and while there, filmed two shows from the TV screen. When the cassette returned from developing she was shocked to find superimposed faces, mirage-like effects on outdoor scenes, and a bizarre image which she interpreted as a 'monk' in death-agony holding a flute-like rod. Tucked into the margin of a frame of Mrs. C's curtains was another bearded cowled face.

On other occasions Stella has found a bright clock-like pattern superimposed across the frames of whatever she was filming, like overhead planes for example. The enlarged details of which have resembled 'flying saucer' shapes and BVM-type light flashes.

Throughout the history of psychic photography there have been many attempts to photograph the human aura, a hypothetical field of energy that extends beyond the physical body forming a luminous envelope. Like Kirlian photography, it was hoped that this would lead to a useful diagnostic tool, since the aura's size, shape and color depended on the physical condition. Interestingly, it was also claimed that the aura responded to mental control and could be molded and extended achieving effects at a distance from the body (remote healing?).

This is one possible mechanism for thoughtography,

psychokinesis is another. Professor Tomokichi Fukurai, of the Imperial University, Tokyo, was a leading Japanese psychic researcher who tested many psychics between 1910 and 1913. One of his subjects, a female with a secondary personality called 'The Goblin', could mentally imprint calligraphic characters onto plates sealed in light proof wrappings. Another of Fukurai's mediums developed a remarkable control and could project two halves of a character onto different plates that would then match up.

In 1949, a Soviet couple, Semyon and Valentia Kirlian, patented a camera-less method of photography. Objects placed directly onto the film within a high frequency electrical field are surrounded by bright discharges, which some believe could be the life-force itself made visible. One Kirlian researcher, Harry Oldfield, took the glowing core from the center of an onion, and photos taken at intervals show it becoming less vibrant as it died.

It is claimed the Kirlian photography shows up the differences between health-giving and junk foods. Similarly, it seems the vital nourishing energy of vegetables is diminished by cooking.

The medium Matthew Manning has several times demonstrated an ability to control the extent of the discharges from his fingertips reinforcing the idea that the images reflect some part of the human energy field. Among the startling experiments by Oldfield is the one conducted on two samples of rock from a roadside wall in Ireland: one from the reputedly haunted site of a fatal coaching accident and the other sample taken further along the road. The haunted rock is darker and displays less vibrant colors than the other rock.

While I understand that this area of Kirlian photography doesn't exactly fit into the category of 'spirit' photography it needs to be explored, because this borders more on the realm of psychic photography. In other words, someone or some energy effecting the film. Years ago I acquired a Kirlian photography apparatus but have never tried or attempted any Kirlian work. The field is indeed fascinating and some interesting results are possible, however I have tried to focus my energies on the area of actual spirit photography instead.

Many people may remember the old paranormal television series *That's Incredible* hosted by John Davidson, Cathy Lee Crosby and Fran Tarkenton, the football great. They usually approached their episodes regarding the paranormal with seriousness and sincerity. Many episodes dealt with spirit photographs and actual evidence collected by their researchers or outside investigators. One episode in particular caught my eye.

In Sunnyvale, California an ordinary Toys 'R Us was allegedly haunted. Employees often complained that toys moved around or fell off the shelves by themselves, while others felt uneasy, especially after the store was closed or before it opened in the morning while they were stocking the shelves. Chills and cold spots were an often occurring phenomena in certain sections of the large store. This was a bit unusual in sunny California!

They began to conduct their own research and soon discovered that the property where the store was built used to be a farm. One farmhand, a young boy, named John Johnston was out chopping wood one day when he fatally cut into one of his legs and he slowly bled to death. Medical doctors often describe bleeding to death as a slow, sort of, draining sensation. So perhaps Johnston doesn't realize that he had in fact died on that fateful day.

That's Incredible, in conjunction with the Toys 'R Us, contacted local California psychic Sylvia Brown. Eyewitnesses to various events, along with Brown and a professional cameraman Bill Tidrow, sat quietly in an empty aisle of the store after closing hours. Tidrow had two cameras set on tripods. One of the cameras was loaded with high-speed infrared film and the other was equipped with a very fast high-speed film that could take photographs in almost total darkness.

Brown then began to make telepathic contact with the ghost and tried to coax him down the aisle where the crew was assembled. A number of pictures were taken that evening during various phases of Brown's seance. When the film was developed, nothing out of the ordinary was seen on any of the normal high-speed photographs. However, on one particular infrared picture, a very clear image of a shadowy figure is seen, hands in his pockets, leaning against a rack of toys at the end of the aisle! According to those partaking in the experiment and seance, there was absolutely no one standing in that location at the time the pictures were taken. In fact, no one was standing at all during the entire process besides those taking the pictures behind the cameras! This is a perfect example of something or someone appearing on only the infrared photograph and NOT the high-speed film taken at precisely the same second!

One of the first good examples of a spirit photograph that I received from an SX-70 camera was sent to me from a woman in November of 1982. Her story goes as follows:

"Enclosed please find the picture of my Grandmothers grave died April, 1934 at age 83. I thought at first it may have been a double exposure but that would hardly be possible as this is a Polaroid Camera that shoots the picture out of the front as soon as it snaps....

".....after I took this one, I took another, clear as a bell (which I sent to my cousin in California) and then the camera would not work. Four more shots were left in the camera. None of them

came out of the camera, yet the film changed and clicked off each shot taken.

"To me if looks like the spirit is coming completely out of the grave, and not on the left side, it looks like a skull?"

After thorough examination of the picture, I was able to bring out much more. There actually appears to be at least two separate individuals within the fog of the picture. First is an older boy with dark hair and a blue shirt with some kind of insignia on it holding a younger girl on his lap who has light brown hair. The boy's right arm, dressed in a short-sleeve shirt, actually trails out of frame slightly left of center. The younger girl is apparently holding something in her lap, which could either be a stuffed or live animal.

These are truly amazing images that were not seen with the naked eye at the time they were photographed but later (within 60 seconds) viewed by the female picture-taker. I have the original SX-70 print in my collection. This picture is one of several that appears on the Ghost Research Society website.

The next several are very distinct semi-transparent and range to a more solid-looking figure. These types of photographs are extremely hard to come by and are considered a once-in-a-lifetime picture. However, if you are quite lucky, you might run across several of them, as I did by having my own website and offering to look at alleged ghost pictures.

This photograph was taken by Jackie Rhame of Florian, Alabama during a visit to a Six Flags Great America Amusement Park in Arlington, Texas. The camera used was a very simple, fix-focused C-126 and the weather conditions were misting rain and quite humid outside. Jackie was just taking a picture of the Texas Giant, the largest roller coaster in the park from a distance. The resulting image clearly shows a semi-transparent figure of a little boy superimposed in the grass wearing a red sweater and possibly a white shirt with a collar beneath.

This picture, during analysis, showed no signs of deliberate double-exposure and that would be a little harder to do with the older style camera she was using at the time. 35mm cameras can obtain a double image easier than either a 110 or 126 camera. There is no known history of this area that might explain who the little boy is nor if there were any fatalities either during construction of the park or any patrons who might have been killed while riding on any attraction inside the park. It's a very frustrating part of ghost research; trying to explain a possible ghostly image and connect it to a trauma, tragedy or untimely death in the past.

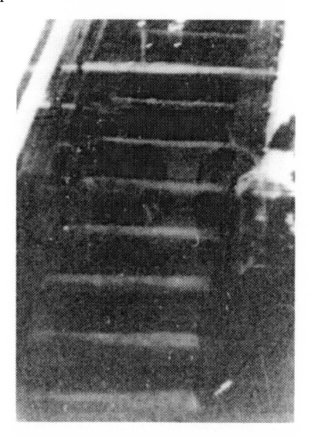

This next image, I'm proud to say, I personally took at Hull House in downtown Chicago in November of 1980 during an investigation of the house and property one evening. Hull House has a rich history of ghost lore dating back to the time of Jane Addams and Ellen Gates Starr, founders of the Hull House projects. Originally built in 1856 for Charles Hull, the house was later discovered by Addams and Starr in 1886 as a run-down tenement house.

The occupants warned Addams and Starr to always leave a picture of water at the top stair leading to the attic, otherwise the ghost from the attic could come downstairs and cause havoc. They were employing the old superstition that ghosts can't cross water. Similar to the story written by Washington Irving, *The Legend of Sleepy Hollow*, where Icabod Crane would be chased by the headless ghost only to finally be safe once he crossed the river bridge.

There were numerous reports coming to the attention of Addams and Starr of semi-transparent figures of women dressed in white who would float and drift in the upstairs hallway before vanishing into a solid door or wall. Some of these accounts came from people attending social events held at the building from time to time. There were also reports of strange fires that would mysteriously break out in one particular upstairs room. Blue plumes of flames would suddenly shoot up out of the floorboards and not scorch anything nearby even though there were draperies, linens, rugs and other combustible material nearby. Often they would simply go out by themselves.

To date strange monk-like figures have been seen peering down from the two upper left-hand windows on the second floor. Seen by motorists, pedestrians, college students and faculty, even though the building is locked up tighter than a drum at night and is only patrolled by campus security from the outside.

It's perhaps these same monk-like figures that I was lucky enough to capture during our mini-investigation of the area back in 1980. A Canon AE-1 camera loaded with black and white infrared film shot at 400 ASA was used for the shoot. The camera was aimed at the stair case and no flash was used, just existing light. Nothing out of the ordinary was either seen or felt that particular evening. However, I got quite a shock when the film was processed!

There, standing on the last five steps of the beautiful red-carpeted stairway were four indistinct, semi-transparent figures. One of them, which is superimposed in the banister, appears to have no head! Two other figures to the extreme left of the stairway of varying heights possible due to the actual steps they were standing on and their own height in feet and inches. But most assuredly the one figure in the center of picture is of extreme interest to me. It resembles that of a monk! A dark figure apparently cowled in monk's attire and a whitish face peering from behind the shroud, his two hands extending from the robe and locked together in prayer. Of course this was not seen as I took the photographs otherwise I would have snapped away like crazy!

There are also some unusual lights directly behind the figures on the stairs, which for all the world look like candles. Perhaps there are still some other, yet indiscernible figures further up the stairs who are carrying the candles? Are these the figures that have been consistently reported by many for quite a number of years? Have they finally reached the bottom of the stairs now and roam freely throughout the building at night? Of course the docents at Hull House vehemently deny any of the ghost stories at Hull House, except those written about in Addams' memoirs and her autobiography, as well as other old books from the time. If they agree with the older stories, why not keep a more open mind on some of the contemporary tales and reports from the more recent past?

Not only have shadowy figures been photographed here in the past but others who have purchased tickets on my bus tours, *Excursions Into The Unknown,* have sometimes taken unusual pictures themselves including strange lights in the building at night, the apparent movement of draperies and blinds upstairs, green glowing fogs and mists somewhat resembling a person climbing the stairs to unusual fogging in the immediate vicinity of the staircase.

One particular set of images come to mind. A woman decided to try her luck at photographing the staircase on one of my Halloween tours. She used a 35mm camera and took two pictures as I often suggest. One with a flash and one without a flash. Just to be sure that you don't bounce the flash off a highly reflective surface. (There is plenty of existing light inside the building even at night to take good photographs without a flash or through the use of a tripod.)

The flash picture showed nothing unusual at all however the picture taken without a flash clearly depicts a strange bluish-white foggy mist all over the middle to upper portion of the staircase. Just the opposite of what you might expect from the two shots. You might think your chances are better for causing a fogging of the film or flash bounce while using a flash rather than not. Nevertheless, I couldn't explain that and it remains two more unexplained images taken at Hull House. When you happen to be in the city, please do visit the building particularly at night and try your luck at capturing something. Hull House is located at 800 S. Halsted Avenue or at the corner of Halsted and Polk directly on the campus of the University of Illinois, Chicago Circle Campus.

One of the most documented images currently in the Ghost Research Society collection is the picture taken by Jude Huff-Felz while she and her sister, Marie Huff, were members of the Ghost Research Society. During a planned investigation of Bachelor's Grove Cemetery on August 10, 1991 a most unusual photograph was taken by Jude.

As you probably know by now, Bachelor's Grove Cemetery, located on the Midlothian Turnpike just east of Ridgeland Avenue, across from Rubio Woods Forest Preserve in south suburban Midlothian, Illinois is the most haunted cemetery or place in the world, according to this author. The area was settled around 1830 with the cemetery being created around 1864. The last official burial was in 1965 and that headstone is still missing today.

There have been grave robberies, destruction of graves, stones and graffiti throughout the years. Bodies, probably due to the gangster era of the 1920s, were found in the lagoon and evidence of Satanic worship in the mid-1960s all stirred together create a most haunted and spooky location.

Tales too numerous to mention have happened throughout the years (but probably beginning in the 1950s) include phantom cars, houses and animals, blue ghost lights, apparitions of a farmer and his horse, a woman carrying a child in her arms, and numerous photographs that have been obtained by professionals and amateurs alike.

On that August day in 1991 about ten members of the GRS were given maps of the cemetery and were told to simply walk on a suggested path through the cemetery, which were marked on the maps. They were told to jot down any sensations, audible, visual, olfactory or where the instruments they were carrying gave off any unusual energy readings or spikes. When one person stopped to record their impressions, the rest of the group directly behind them also stopped. This prevented any cross-contamination or coercion of data. Only after all had been through the route were the maps cross-referenced for possible collective "hits" or areas where several people had had an encounter or equipment reaction of some kind.

It soon became apparent that a small checkerboard tombstone with no discernible name on it was one of several areas where a number of people had felt uncomfortable. According to standard protocol, we immediately re-visited those suspect areas and took additional readings and began photographic experiments.

Two in the group were using black and white infrared film but it was the Huff-Felz camera that captured the unusual image on the checkerboard tombstone. The image reproduced in this book is an enlargement of the original photograph done so for clarity purposes. It shows a semi-transparent figure of a woman in an old-fashioned, turn-of-the-century-styled dress, sitting on the tombstone in profile, staring off into the distance. She appears to have long dark brown, shoulder-length hair with her hands gently resting on her legs.

The image is a bit fuzzy but later analysis indicates that parts of her body are truly see-through including the area of her head and feet. Parts of trees and nearby foliage can be seen through the woman's image. Since the woman's image is at rest and rules out movement by the subject, it indicates that the subject "isn't all there" and that's only a manner of speaking. Obviously no one of our group or anyone visiting the cemetery that day was dressed in that kind of attire, as anyone of our members would have noticed someone costumed in a long flowing dress out in the middle of Cook County Forest Preserves. To present I have no idea who the figure represents but the logical explanation is someone buried at Bachelor's Grove and is not at rest for whatever reason that may be.

This photograph has been subjected to intense scrutiny not only by myself and other members of the Ghost Research Society but the general public as well because it did make its way into the *Chicago Sun-Times* and the *National Examiner* around Halloween of that year. While some who responded didn't believe it to be a real ghost, the majority had very positive responses and felt that it must be a ghost. I have full faith in Huff-Felz and the development process of the infrared film and do not believe in the slightest to be a hoax or natural explanation.

The picture was however picked about on a Discovery Channel documentary entitled *"Phantom Photographs"*, where it was submitted to "alleged" experts at Kodak for their findings and analysis. One gentleman, who shall remain nameless, suggested that he believed it to be a real person based on the fact that the image cast a shadow on the ground around the tombstone and the gravestone itself. However, if you look closely at the image, there are shadows all around the gravestone indicating the image and stone to have been partly in the shadows cast by the nearby trees and foliage. So much for that theory.... Besides that, they could not come up with any other possible explanation for the image other to say that if it was a ghost, does a ghost cast a shadow? Good question!

However, the one haunting image that remains my favorite and most unexplainable to date would have to be the ordinary picture taken on a sunny afternoon in Chicago of a woman and a child posing in front of the new home they had just moved into. It was taken by husband and there were no other people either inside or outside the house at the time. A 35mm camera was used and nothing was seen or felt during the picture-taking process.

After the film was developed, two eerie faces show up in the doorway behind the mother and her child. The face on the left appears to be that of an older woman with her hair pulled up in a bun with dark sunken eyelets for eyes. Directly to the right of the woman is a floating face of a dog, a bulldog in particular. Short cropped ears and a large pushed-in nose, characteristic of a bulldog are clearly visible. Remember there were no people or animals in the house at the time of the shooting.

When I first got the call from, let us call her Dora, she wanted to show me the picture immediately and would not even trust the

U.S. Postal Service with the delivery. She actually handed me the original picture and explained the circumstances. There had been no paranormal activity in the house prior or since the picture was taken. Dora did state that the face of the woman looked a great deal like one of her relatives that had died before she had a chance to meet them. The resemblance was uncanny! There was no history of an animal, or bulldog, in any of her family. Perhaps the animal resides there from a previous owner?

This picture was also scrutinized by so-called experts from Kodak on that same Discovery Channel documentary. They claimed the images were reflections from a person or persons (animals) somewhere slightly off of the center of where the picture was taken. They further tried to argue that there are similar images in the windows to the extreme right of the photo. I disagree!

If you look closely at the faces, if they are reflections, they would have to be reflected individually into the different panes of the storm door as these are individual panes of glasses which open up independent of one another. There are even curious "white collars" at the bottom of each face, which most likely are reflections from the sunlight. However, to suggest that each face was meticulously reflected into such a recognizable face, is utter nonsense.

But remember, it's always easier to explain away an image than it is to explain it. You will run across this scenario all the time as you attempt to analyze your own pictures or those of others. I never had the opportunity to debunk the debunkers on the show. So, it looked to all the world that the experts were right. Well, you make your own decision now that you have all the facts concerning this picture.

Another curiosity in this picture, and it's a bit hard to see, (go to the website for more clarity), are the anomalous little blue faces that appear to run horizontally from the area of the steps and stop on the belly of the child. Very close examination of these curiosities show that they truly resemble little blue faces. I don't believe them to be a chemical spill or a flaw in the development process. I'm not actually suggesting that they ARE real tiny blue faces but they sure do appear to be. I just cannot find another natural explanation for them to date.

-CONCLUSION-

I sincerely hope the images in the last couple of chapters, whether they be natural or supernatural, have given you a better understanding of what to look for when analyzing or simply viewing alleged paranormal pictures. Remember the Ghost Research Society is always ready, willing and able to help and assist you in any way, free of charge, if you stumble upon something that you simply cannot explain.

In wrapping up this book, let us quickly go over some valid points and areas to avoid and what to look for. This is not THE definitive book on spirit photography but I've tried to put forth methods that have worked for me and the other GRS members in the past. If you only learn one or two things from this book that will help you in the future, then it's been a success for me.

Always use more than one camera in your investigations and experimentations and try to have an instant camera handy for feeling around subjected areas that might yield good results with the 35mm cameras.

While digital cameras are fine for a variety of reasons, including the ability to see instantly what you have taken, they should never be used solo because of the unexpected results (orbs) that they are known to produce. In conjunction with other instant or 35mm cameras is really the way to go with this new technology.

If you plan to use infrared film, make sure it is purchased from a reputable dealer and is removed from a refrigerator. If it isn't, don't buy it! It probably isn't good. This film must be loaded and unloaded in TOTAL darkness and not in subdued light and shot up as quickly as possible.

While Kodak recommends certain filters to be used with certain films, including infrared, the key word is experimentation. See what works best for you and stay with it. But constantly experiment with different ideas until you come up with a method that produces consistent results.

The faster the film, the better when attempting spirit photography since that will allow you to shoot in almost total darkness without the use of flash photography, which could produce unwanted flash bounce or glare that might be mistaken for a ghostly image. The use of tripods under low-light conditions is a must! Tripods are very inexpensive and should be employed most of the time to minimize camera shake and blurred images.

The use of 'ghost hunting' equipment might better your chances of localizing an area to photograph rather than simply shooting images at random all over the place. The ones I suggest should be mandatory in everyone's arsenal and include a good EMF, temperature and humidity gauge, and an electrostatic detector of some kind. These areas of research are the most often recorded in conjunction and association with paranormal phenomena. If you cannot afford these, then use an animal like a cat or dog and see how they react while being brought into a haunted area.

Camcorders, especially those with nightvision capabilities, should be employed at all times and can even be used in addition and at the same time as your experimentation with digital, instant and 35mm cameras. That is even a better way to convince those skeptical debunkers that your methods are on the up and up and you have just made a video log of your investigation or experimentation.

Design forms for your group such as one for picture-taking and another for analysis and keep those handy at all times. This will refresh your memory of the exact circumstances at the time of your photography session.

Patience is very important in this work. As you might go through dozens of rolls of film before you obtain your first paranormal image. Don't give up! You might be lucky earlier than later but continue your experiments and make the necessary changes to your protocol until you begin to photograph strange and unexplainable images.

Never smoke or allow anyone to smoke at any photographic session. If filming outside in the cold, hold your breath while taking pictures or use a tripod and cable release and face away from the camera when you snap the picture.

Be aware of the weather conditions; temperature, humidity, solar information and the location where you are filming. Is it near high tension electrical wires? Are you near a stream of running water? Are there drastic temperature differences between where your camera is and what you are attempting to photograph? What is the insect population where you are filming? Are you near a highway at night with oncoming and receding headlights or taillights? Always, always be completely aware of your surroundings at all times.

Remove or wear your camera or wrist straps so that they do not dangle in front of the lens. Keep your fingers and any other obstructions well behind the lens of the camera, especially if you don't own a 35mm with a TTL viewfinder.

Keep your group small and quiet and always leave the area as you found it, in pristine condition. Don't remove souvenirs! And don't leave behind trash, film canisters and boxes or even your lunch litter. That's the surest way not to get an invite again.

Never go alone to anywhere, even in broad daylight. There's safety in numbers and you could miss something that someone else in your group might catch. Plus, it's easier for a group to help you lug your equipment around in a reasonable amount of time.

Never buy the "bargain brand" tape or outdated film at a discount. You're just asking for trouble and unexpected results. Sometimes the film won't even develop properly. Invest a little more and stay with name brands like Kodak, Fuji, Agfa, etc.

Make sure the lens is cleaned before each investigation or experiment and if you are going in and out in cold weather conditions, allow the equipment to warm properly to prevent fogging of the film, or lens.

If you follow these simple rules you will soon see some results. Good luck to you!!

BIBLIOGRAPHY

Basics of Camera Operation

Kodak Filters for Scientific and Technical Uses (1981)
Master Photography: Take and Make Perfect Pictures by
Michael Busselle (1977)

Films and Their Uses

Kodak Infrared Films (1976)
Ultraviolet & Fluorescence Photography (1972)

Digital Cameras

Digital Cameras - or, Ghost Hunting at its Worst by
Troy Taylor http://www.prairieghosts.ocm

Analysis of Your Spirit or Non-spirit Images

*Ghost That Haunts 300-year-old Church Poses for
Photograph* by Crandall McIntosh (Sun) 4-21-87

Lview Pro diagnostic software http://www.lview.com
VuePrint Pro diagnostic software http://hamrick.com

<u>Suggested Further Reading & Viewing</u>

An Unknown Encounter (Video 1997)

Evidence For Spirit Photography by Dale Kaczmarek
(Pursuit Journal, Vol. 19, No. 1, 1986)

Ghosts and How to See Them by Peter Underwood (1993)

Handbook of Unusual Natural Phenomena by William R. Corliss
(1977)

Photographing the Invisible by James Coates (1973)

*Photographing the Spirit World: Images From Beyond the
Spectrum* by Cyril Permutt (1988)

Photographs of the Unknown by Robert Rickard & Richard Kelly
(1980)

Psychic Photography: Threshold of a New Science? by Hans Holzer
(1970) reprinted as *America's Restless Ghosts* (1993)

Real Ghost Hunters, Discovery Channel (Video 1999)

- ABOUT THE AUTHOR -
DALE KACZMAREK

Dale Kaczmarek is the President of the Ghost Research Society, and international organization of ghost researchers that is based in the Chicago area. He is also author of WINDY CITY GHOSTS (the original book) and the editor of a number of publications about ghosts and hauntings including *National Register of Haunted Locations, Bibliography of Ghost Movies, Ghostly Websites* and others.

He has also contributed to and appeared in a number of occult-related books including *Dead Zones* by Sharon Jarvis, *The Encyclopedia of Ghosts and Spirits* by Rosemary Ellen Guiley, *More Haunted Houses* by Joan Bingham and Dolores Riccio, *Haunted Places: The National Directory* by Dennis William Hauck, *Sightings* by Susan Michaels and many others.

Dale has made a number of television appearances on local and national news programs and has appeared in many documentaries and shows about ghosts and haunted places including *Real Ghosthunters, Sightings, Encounters, The Other Side, Mysteries, Magic and Miracles, A.M. Chicago* (with Oprah Winfrey) and many others. He has also appeared on dozens of radio programs as well.

In addition to serving as president of the Ghost Research Society, Dale is also a member of the American Association Electronic Voice Phenomena (AA-EVP), International Fortean Organization (INFO), Society for the Investigation of the Unexplained (SITU) and Honorary Lifetime Member of the Ghost Society of England.

He is also the host of the highly recommended *Excursions Into The Unknown Tours* of the Chicagoland area, the only full-time, year-round bus tour in the Chicagoland area. He currently resides with his wife Ruth in Oak Lawn.

Printed in the United States
70550LV00006B/453